THE DIALECTICS OF LITERARY CONSCIOUSNESS

THE DIALECTICS OF LITERARY CONSCIOUSNESS

KRISHNAN KUTTY

PARTRIDGE
A Penguin Random House Company

To order additional copies of this book, contact
Partridge India
000 800 10062 62
orders.india@partridgepublishing.com

www.partridgepublishing.com/india

CONTENTS

FOREWORD

For my B.A. (English Literature) degree course, I remember, the Social and Literary History of England was a subsidiary paper. G. M. Trevelyan's book on the subject was one of the reference books. But the class room transaction did not go beyond references to social issues in the works of major authors. Only when I began to study Marxism, I could properly account for its function and relevance in literature.

My serious introduction to Marxian Aesthetics took place outside the academia. I happened to attend a school on Marxism, organized by a collective of left-oriented associations of college teachers, in 1979, at Alwaye, where late P. Govinda Pillai spoke about Raymond Williams and the Frankfurt School philosophers. Aesthetically, he fortified my understanding of dialectical and historical materialism the basics of which I had already gathered from the works of E.M.S.Namboodiripadu, the first Marxist Chief Minister of Kerala, and Dr.M.P. Parameswaran, one of the pioneers of the People's Science Movement in India. I wish to acknowledge my indebtedness to these three formative figures of intellectual and political life in modern Kerala.

The book is a witness of my effort to come to grips with Marxian Literary Aesthetics. The chapters of this book were originally prepared on different occasions for various university seminars. In collecting them now, the purpose is to highlight the principle of dialectics at work in writing, reading, interpretation and translation.

But for the repeated prodding and prompt responses of Mr.Adraian Kane and Ms Gemma Ramos of Partridge Publishing Company, I would not have succeeded in giving these articles the book form they have now. I thank them sincerely.

I wish to place on record my gratitude to Prof. K.S. Sreekala, my former colleague in the Department of English, Government College, Kottayam, for her critical review of the manuscripts. Also I wish to state my appreciation of the scrutiny that Nikhil Krishnan, my younger son, did with the first chapter of the book, "Literary Consciousness: A Dialectical and Historical Introduction". He purged it of its superfluity. Akhil Krishnan, my nephew, prepared the index to the book. I acknowledge his service and admire his skill.

I wish to thank my friend Dr.K.Ramachandran, former Registrar, Sree Sankaracharya University of Sanskrit, Kalady, for suggesting the idea for the book cover. Also I sincerely thank Mr. George Mathew, Grace Graphics, Pathanamthitta, Kerala for the beautiful realization of the cover and for the meticulous lay out and settings of the book.

Above all, I place on record the support of my wife Dr. V.R.Vijayalekshmi, my best critic and mentor.

Krishnan Kutty

LITERARY CONSCIOUSNESS:

A DIALECTICAL AND HISTORICAL INTRODUCTION

Dialectical and historical materialism, the encapsulation of Marxian world view, is the logical culmination of the development of philosophical thought through successive human generations. As no other philosophy has done, Marxism has radically revolutionized the concept of Consciousness. The principles of dialectical and historical materialism have integrated the human understanding of Nature, History and Consciousness. Marxian dialectics incessantly deepens itself with the latest knowledge in scientific disciplines. It provides total understanding of objective reality and accounts for all forms of material manifestations and mental processes, including imaginative expressions. An instrument for the practical reconstruction of society, it objectively assesses the historical requirements of social revolution. Therefore, despite the persistent denigration by vested interests, dialectical and historical materialism acts as an effective antidote to the vague abstractions and ideological mystifications of Idealism. It is a comprehensive system of philosophy that offers sustained intellectual satisfaction.

Karl Marx and Friedrich Engels applied the Hegelian laws of dialectics - the transformation of quantity into quality and vice versa, the interpenetration of the opposites and the negation of negation - as the "algebra of revolution."[1] Conceptually and practically, they revolutionized the fundamentals of philosophy. They wanted philosophy to change the world, not merely interpret it. They discarded the idealistic content of Hegelian dialectics and enunciated their materialist principles of existence and epistemology. Contradiction, the chief category of dialectics, is the key to natural and historical processes and developments.

Prior to the rational formulation of dialectical and historical materialism, for centuries, idealist philosophers dealt with consciousness as something inscrutable and mysterious. They abstracted it away from human body and assigned it extra-material existence, identity and immutability. They called it soul, an invisible vapor that animated the human body and survived death. They attributed transcendence to it, bestowed it with providential powers and called it God or Allah or Universal Spirit or Grand Idea or Brahman. In diverse idealistic ways they rationalized their irrationality and superstition.

Dialectical materialism has logically explained the nature, origin and function of consciousness which is one of the basic questions of philosophy and with which all scientists and philosophers have been greatly concerned. It considers consciousness to be "a derivative of matter", "one of the specific manifestations of the social form of the motion of matter".[2] Marxist dialectical materialism, basing its arguments on Darwin's Theory of Evolution, has given rational insights into the nature of human consciousness. Human brain and language are the consequences of material evolution at the biological and sociological levels. The exciting history of the origin of life and the evolution of man has provided materialist dialectics the scientific credential to refute the divine theory of creation. There are many physiological features which distinguish human beings from other animals. Man, the most advanced of all animals, now sits logically pretty at the topmost branch of the tall Tree of Evolution. He is a biped that can stand erect, turn its head and look about. He has long agile hands with flexible fingers. He can walk and talk and run fast. If necessary, he can stand still or lie down on his back and scan the sky for stars. Over and above all these, man can cry and laugh and think. He has language. He has consciousness. Consciousness *tells* man that he is *man*.

Man is of nature and, yet, different from it. Whereas all other animals are totally dependent on nature, man has partly mastered it and enjoys comparative independence. He is not a mere fruit or root gatherer or a predator, but a producer who transforms nature to suit his purpose. Concurrently, man is dependent on and independent of nature. The freedom that man has achieved from nature is the handiwork of two of his highly developed physical organs-the hand and the brain. Man has hands, the organ for work, and has brain, the organ for thought. The two interact and dialectically influence each other. Tools, the result of the influence of mind on hand, help man transform nature. As Engels has said, human beings have impressed "the stamp of their will upon the earth"[3]. Man impacts on nature and is impacted on by it too.

Human consciousness, the result of man's dialectical relationship to nature and society, manifests itself in language, an arbitrary signaling system. The science of biological evolution has established that, physiologically, human beings have developed in such a way as to make speech and language possible. Human vocal tract is unique among animals. It is differently shaped and much larger than that of apes. To the apes the epiglottis is a valve between the trachea and the esophagus. When raised, the trachea is connected to the nose and the mouth is sealed off. But in humans, pharynx is common for both the flow of air and the passage of food. The vocal tracts of chimpanzees are shaped like those of new born human babies. But after three months, the trachea of the human child changes in size with increased pharyngeal area. Slowly the child begins to articulate sounds into vowels and consonants. Whereas the chimpanzee can produce only one or two vowel sounds, the human adult, with large and elongated vocal tract, can produce a variety of sounds.

Recent neuro-linguistic studies have confirmed the role of human brain in the production of language. The comparison of the features of the brains of apes and humans has proved that apes lack that part of the brain which enables speech. The human brain, the product of thousands of years of biological evolution, has acquired the distinct faculty of language as a dialectical consequence of using hands dexterously. It is conjectured that the small brain of the early chimpanzees got cumulatively enlarged as a result of the frequent employment of hands. The transition of *Homo erectus* first to *Homo habilis,* and then to *Homo sapiens,* was due to labor, manual and collective. All sights, seen and shown, and all sounds, spoken and heard, were for food or shelter and they were sought and found collectively. Language, the dialectical offshoot of the collective labor phase in social history, has the human brain as its matrix.

It is common experience that those who suffer from paralytic strokes or suffocation or accidents or injuries show symptoms of Aphasia. The clotting of blood in the small blood vessels of the brain causes the quick death of the tissues and the loss of power of speech. The patient loses the ability to use language properly. The authoritative studies of Paul Broca and Carl Wernick into Aphasia have confirmed that human brain, the most sophisticated form of matter, is the center of linguistic operations. Language is the result of diverse electro-chemical processes in human brain. Positron Emission Tomography has made possible the charting of the processes in the human brain while it uses language. Modern science and medical technology have dismissed the myths regarding the origin of language.

That language is primarily meant to communicate is a broad statement of its collective origin. Outside society, there is no language or thought. Only when man reflects nature and collaborates in productive labor, he needs to think or speak or write. Language enables man to communicate his feelings, sensations, experiences, ideas and thoughts with others. Besides, language helps him think and store ideas in his brain and retrieve them from there at will. Language is the software of the brain matter. A live human body is inevitable for its function. Brain is primary and consciousness (thought) is secondary. There is no consciousness without a living brain. Mental functions are functions of body, living matter. There is no idea without matter. Mind is matter, a unique product of biological evolution. Therefore, thought is a construct of matter. Matter is primary and idea secondary. Logically, thus, Marx made philosophy stand upright on its feet. Consciousness is always conscious existence - a distinctive functional relationship in which human mind keeps itself in dialogue with the external world and its mental reflections.

Dialectical and historical materialism considers human labor a seminal factor that structures social reality. The interventions of man in the processes of nature through labor affect nature and man dialectically. All sorts of knowledge, wealth and culture are the cumulative upshots of social labor. True to its proletarian character, dialectical and historical materialism analyzes the inter-relationship of human hands, tools, work, society, nature, brain and thought. Also it considers how labor has contributed to the evolution of consciousness. All labor is social labor. Hands are natural tools of man and, using them skillfully, he produces imaginatively tools for new labor situations. He works on nature with hands and tools. Tools, the extensions to human limbs, are the dialectical products of human manual work. Manual labor has made man different from other beasts. With the invention of tools and their progressive innovation, rapid qualitative changes have taken place in the interrelationships of man, nature and society. The historical transition of human society from primitive savagery through slavery, feudalism and capitalism to scientific socialism is marked by revolutionary jumps in the quality of tools for economic production. Social evolution is marked by progressive evolution of human consciousness too. In primitive societies as labor was always collective, consciousness was social and collective in origin. Over a period of time, qualitative changes in social relationships paved the way for the evolution of socialist moral consciousness, central to the philosophy of dialectical and historical materialism.

Friedrich Engels has clearly elucidated the labor theory of consciousness in the *Dialectics of Nature*: "It [Labor] is the prime basic condition for all human existence, and this to such an extent that, in a sense, we have to say that labor created man himself."[4] Many anthropologists and Darwinian evolutionists have pointed out that the origin of language should be related to the evolution of man as tool maker. As the areas of the brain, which control the organs of speech and hands, are adjacent, quite possibly, they influence each other. Thus, dialectically, manual labor has affected human brain, enabling the articulation of speech. The encryption of brain with language marks the genesis of consciousness. "*Labor has made man and human society.* It was precisely in Labor, in productive activity that man's brain, his consciousness developed…. Consciousness is the product of man's life in society. It is a social phenomenon."[5]

Briefly put, Marxism considers objective social reality as the source-nursery of consciousness. Marx has substantiated the dialectical genesis and process of human consciousness, thus: "It is not the consciousness of men that determines their being, but, on the contrary, their social being that determines their consciousness."[6] Those people who have not understood 'dialectics' properly have criticized that Marxian concept of consciousness suffers from economic determinism because Marx has theorized that social being determines it. In fact dialectics has the answer to this criticism also. The conscious or self-aware man always strives, with inevitable dialectical consequences, to transform natural and social reality in accordance with the requirements of his life. Imagination, a faculty of the human brain, enables man to negotiate reality, the factors which control his natural and social being. It sets forth an endless repetitive process of thesis-antithesis-synthesis in its dialogue with reality. In politics, in poetry and in every human operation imagination plays a creative role. The individual, seized with imagination, considers the historical past and contemporary reality and visualizes the future. An element of criticism of the past and the present is implicit in it. Also there is an effort "to transform a previous experience and create new ideas and images, linking up the existent with the absent" and "the sensual and the rational in cognition"[7].

The only manifest outputs of human consciousness are signs, verbal and visual. All signs, natural or artificial, are the result of man-nature dialectics. Language, an arbitrary system of verbal signs, enables man to think, to be self-aware and to communicate with others through speech and writing. It actualizes thought; it abstracts and generalizes perceptions and experiences; it reflects reality; and it enables creative reflection on reality. Language, social in origin, enables dialectical interaction within society, bonding and building cohesion. Man, the perceiver, and nature, the perceived, unite in perception, an experience abstracted into a concept, a sign. Articulated vowels and consonants arbitrarily constitute the sign system of language. For communication, either verbal or visual or audio-visual signs are employed. The progressive evolution and increasing complexity in the use of signs has been concurrent in the historical evolution of human consciousness. Human consciousness is, thus, a composite semiotic phenomenon which does not allow easy analysis and apprehension.

Literary art employs linguistic signs connotatively for purposes different from factual or denotative communication. Though the signs of language and literature are identical, their semantic functions differ qualitatively. Generally, linguistic signs represent human perceptions, experiences, ideas, concepts, feelings and emotions; but, their literary use is deviant and imparts them a distinct artistic niche. With their formal uniqueness, linguistic signs exalt themselves to the level of literary art. Aesthetically, they affect and address human consciousness.

Aesthetics is a special branch of philosophy in which human mind negotiates reality in ways subtly different from those of science. In the scientific perception of reality, absolute importance is given to the impersonal and the objective. The scientist's personal preferences or prejudices have no place in the final theoretical generalization arrived at after repeated experimental verifications. Nothing but objective truth has any relevance in science; subjectivity is at zero degree level in science. But, in art, especially in literary art, the personal inclination of the artist reigns supreme. The form, content, genre and style are all decided by the artist. He is the monarch of all he surveys in his world of art. But the distinct nature of art has made most artists megalomaniacs who flatter themselves into the delusive belief that they are divinely blessed and inspired. In fact they wallow in the quagmire of subjective idealism. Theirs is the pathetic spectacle of an unwieldy ego struggling to tackle an unyielding social reality. True, their power of imagination makes them extraordinary. But their distinctive imagination does not make them extraterrestrial. Their faculty is a material phenomenon, an aspect of the human mind, a form of matter. Though uncommon, there is nothing unnatural about it.

Marxian aesthetics has thoroughly revolutionized the entire philosophy of art. Pre-Marxian aesthetic philosophers were idealists who treated creative imagination, as found in poetry and art, to be the consequence of divine inspiration. Anchored on dialectical and historical materialism, Marxian aesthetics has radically transformed the tenets of idealist aesthetics. Like thought, art is another aspect of human consciousness. In essence artistic imagination is materialistic, not spiritual or idealistic. As already noted, imagination is a special faculty of the mind which gets activated on collision with reality. The dialectical artist, cured of the delusive power of idealism, realizes the materialistic base of his trans-creative impulse. He has a new vision, a new world view, and he does not fumble for any divine halo about him. He has a new social personality, evolving dialectically. With every imaginative venture, the artist launches himself forward into the societal future, foregrounding his visions. He relentlessly engages himself in the criticism of the present and the past, reflects on his experiences and strives for the realization of his visions and aspirations in future, in his art, the concrete manifestation of his creative imagination. And, logically, every artistic exercise is a search for another reality, an alternative social being, a new world order. And, therefore, imagination is inherently and potentially political[8]. Every true artist, whether he is conscious or unconscious of it, is a political philosopher. His mission is to spell out his vision in terms of subtle imagination.

Art, like Science, is an exercise in Freedom. The artist and the scientist are differently concerned with reality which defines their freedom. The scientist applies his sense of reason and intellect to take cognizance of reality. But the (literary) artist, emotionally concerned with social reality and the complex nature of human relationships, seeks freedom through flights of imagination. Christopher Caudwell has noted,

> Art is the science of feeling, science the art of knowing. We must know to be able to do, but we must feel to know what to do. Art is born of struggle, because there is in society a conflict between phantasy and reality[9].

According to Caudwell, man has a 'better self', the conscious psyche which is the creation of society. Also in man there is the lingering presence of the genotype, the human animal, the 'worse self'. The history of human evolution is full of long, exciting and, often, tortuous episodes of struggle to shed the 'worse self'. Art facilitates the evolution of human moral consciousness, the assertion of the 'better self'.[10]

Artistic response to the pleasures, frustrations, challenges, excitements, struggles and achievements of life is a way for asserting one's humanness. The freedom to choose one's destiny is decisive in determining the quality and character of one's life. Man is free to choose; but animals are not. This enables man to intuit future and redefine his freedom. The enjoyment of freedom in class society is one of the central themes of Marxism. Marx saw "freedom as man's ability to exercise conscious rational control over his natural environment and over his own social forces"[11]. So far as the bourgeois is concerned, freedom is the autonomous right to indulge in free trade – to trade in human labor and natural resources. The bourgeois concept of freedom is limited by property interests. A socio-economic system, that keeps most people always job-locked, tense and aggressive, cannot fulfill the tenets of freedom. The absence of freedom - the alienation of the worker from the fruit of his labor, the producer from the product - is the root cause of all social evils. The opposition to it gives Marxism an ethical base and a humanistic ground to put forward its imaginative philosophic vision. Marxism strives for freedom from class exploitation and associated complexities which hamper untrammeled development of human personality at the individual and social levels. Marxian literary consciousness is acutely aware of class conflict as decisive in defining human freedom. Creative imagination, usually attributed to art alone, is latent in every form of social praxis, including the scientific and the political. It helps overreach all available forms of existence. A natural ally to freedom, creative imagination helps visualize a future when each human being can pursue any form of art and craft of his choice. The pursuit of freedom to enjoy it in its fullness will dialectically go on *ad infinitum*.

ENDNOTES

1   Aleander Ivanovich Herzen (1812-180), Russian revolutionary materialist. *Dictionary of Philosophy*, 2nd rev. ed. (Moscow: Progress Publishers, 1984) 107.

2   *Fundamentals of Marxist-Leninist Philosophy*, published by Institute of Social Sciences (Moscow: Progress Publishers, 1985)104.

3   Friedrich Engels, "Part Played by Labor in Transition from Ape to Man," *Dialectics of Nature*, rev. ed. (Moscow: Progress Publishers, 1954)179.

4   Friedrich Engels, *Dialectics of Nature*, 170.

5   V.Podostnik and O.Ykhot, *A Brief Course of Dialectical Materialism*, (Moscow: Progress Publishers) n.d.55.

6   Quoted from Marx, "A Contribution to the Critique of Political Economy", Lenin in *Marx, Engels, Marxism,* rpt. (Moscow: Progress Publishers, 1973)18-19.

7   Galina Kirilenko and Lydia Korshunova, *What is Philosophy?* (Moscow: Progress Publishers 1985) 202-203.

8   Edward Bond, "Introduction" to *Bingo: Scenes of Money and Death,* included in *Plays 3* (London: Methuen, 1987) 5.

9   Christorpher Caudwell, *Illusion and Reality*, 1945; rpt. (New Delhi: People's Publishing House, 1956) 280.

10 Christorpher Caudwell, *Illusion and Reality*, 281.

11 Andrezj Walicki, "Marx and Freedom", *the New York Review of Books*, (Nov. 24, 1983)

NATURE AND ENVIRONMENT:

POETIC IMPRINTS OF
SHIFTING PERSPECTIVES

Nature and Environment are not synonyms, but two subtly discrete concepts with different signification. Nature comprises everything including man, but excluding his handiworks, the artificial products of his labor. But conceptually different, Environment signifies the natural surroundings on which man acts and depends on for sustenance and survival. The difference is the result of historical and objective changes in the relationship between man and nature. Though for millions of years man has been using different kinds of implements for collecting food and for ensuring security, the very purpose and function of tools underwent revolutionary changes with the invention of the steam engine and the advent of industrial capitalism. Since then man has invaded and infected every nook and corner of the Earth and transformed it into his environment, the center for his economic activity. As a result of the rampant exploitation of natural resources, environmental hazards have multiplied beyond measure raising questions of human survival on earth. Humanity is at a crisis. Though, since the middle of the nineteenth century, many scientists and sensitive people have been voicing their concern, only after Rachel Carson's *Silent Spring* spoke loud and clear, the leaders of geo-politics have turned their eyes and ears to environmental issues. In fact, English poets were the first to note and inscribe the impact of the exploitation of nature on human sensibility and consciousness. The four centuries of modern English Poetry is a meticulous record of the social and historical processes, accelerated by the fumes of the steam engine and the wheels of industry. The great English poems are historic signposts of the progressive evolution of English Nature poetry to take on the issues of the politics and the poetics of Environment in the postindustrial age.

The Elizabethan Age in English poetry is replete with the sentiments of ageing Feudalism and aspiring Capitalism. Nature provided enough descriptive and figurative material to poets like Sir Thomas Wyatt (1503-1542), Henry Howard, Earl of Surrey (1517-1547) and Edmund Spenser (1552-1599) of early sixteenth-century. As they were basking in the twilight of Feudalism, Nature was still a fine array of woods and rocks and streams and birds and buds and flowers to them. Nature was the source of beautiful experiences, of visual feast and sensual smell and exhilarating music. It offered the Elizabethans enough forms and figures to complement personal feelings or to contemplate on experiences. On Nature then man had no economic design other than that of agricultural production. As natural resources were not tapped for mass industrial production, Nature still provided an ambience to deal with the themes of feudal love and beauty.

Among the Elizabethan poets, Christopher Marlowe (1564-1593) was the first to note the advent of the

Renaissance and, along with it, the increasing aggressive greed for wealth. The spirit of inquiry into the mysteries of Nature had sprouted from the essence of emerging capitalism. Imaginatively, Marlowe responded to the new world beyond the blue sky which was revealed by the astronomers who relentlessly scanned the stars and the space beyond them. Had not Nicolaus Copernicus (1473-1543) stated his revolutionary theory, Marlowe's poetry would not have turned its imaginative vision on the micro and macro structures of the Cosmos. It was a move away from the divinely created geo-centric world full of limits and borders. The new heliocentric view had tremendous philosophical significance. It impacted upon human intellectual and imaginative faculties as nothing else had done before. Marlowe's protagonist speaks of "Nature, that framed us of four elements" and "the wondrous architecture of the world" in the first part of *Tamburlaine the Great* (Act II, scene 7). The spirit of scientific inquiry, that had begun to compel man to redefine his interface with Nature, was a great influence on the adventurous spirit of Marlowe's Tamburlaine[1]. Tamburlaine learns that

> Our souls, whose faculties can comprehend
> The wondrous architecture of the world,
> And measure every wandering planet's course,
> Still climbing after knowledge infinite,...
> Until we reach the ripest fruit of all,
> That perfect bliss and sole felicity,
> The sweet fruition of an earthly crown.
> (*Tamburlaine the Great,* Part I, Act II, Sc.7)

By the time of William Shakespeare (1564-1616), the frantic search for wealth, especially money and gold, had become the prime object of human endeavor, including geographical explorations. So a Merchant of Venice or a Lear or a Timon of Athens or a Prospero had to suffer from conflicting equations of economic and political power. The age was one of expansion and empire building. The dawn of colonial imperialism saw England in a new political and economic glory. There were many seafaring adventurers who brought not only riches but also fanciful and fantastic stories about the far-off places and people that they had discovered during their adventurous voyages. The astrologers and the alchemists of the time shared much of the economic ambition of the rising bourgeoisie. They relentlessly pursued scientific knowledge and sharpened their intellect to gain economic omnipotence. Prospero's words in *The Tempest* (Act V, Scene 1, 34-57) bring out the internecine conflicts in the craze for political power and the pursuit of the secrets of Nature[2]. Prospero's loss of political authority and his isolation on an island cave were the results of his pursuit of the knowledge of Nature which gave him great authority over its elemental forces. He claims to

> … have bedimmed
> The moon-tide sun, call'd forth the mutinous winds
> And 'twixt the green sea and the azur'd vault
> Let roaring war: to the dread rattling thunder
> Have I given fire, and rifted Jove's oak….

Prospero's abjuration of "this rough magic" has the ring of a 21st century environmentalist-turned industrialist's renunciation of his self-destructive conquest of Nature. Though the claim of magical power is an indirect admission of the superiority of natural elements, it is also an expression of the indomitable desire of human beings to master them. But to do that, man has to learn the natural laws and deliberately intervene in the natural processes. The post-Copernican period in human history is an eventful period of continuous Man-Nature interface.

The 17th and 18th centuries are marked by rapid colonial expansion. Many geographical discoveries were conducted during this period. Rising European colonial powers fought many wars at home and abroad for supremacy. Many new races of human beings, new continents, numerous languages and various cultural heritages were discovered. New economic resources were identified and new food for intellectual sustenance was also generated. The map of the world and the contours of the human brain were being re-drawn which had great influence on human imagination. In the metaphysical reflections of John Donne we find the imaginative impact of scientific knowledge:

> Let sea-discoverers to new worlds have gone;
> Let maps to other worlds on worlds have shown;
> Let us possess one world; each hath one, and is
> one ....
> Where can we find two better hemispheres
> Without short north, without declining west?
> ("The Good Morrow",13-19)

In the epic poetry of John Milton (1608-1674), Nature receives a treatment that is devoid of Feudal trimming and trappings. Instead, he employs the natural phenomena to serve his protestant religious purpose— the vindication of the ways of God to Man. Milton was thoroughly informed of the latest in astronomy and cosmology. He had personal acquaintance with Galileo, his great contemporary and the greatest scientist of all times. Just before Galileo's death, during 1638-39, Milton had visited him in Italy. Therefore, he could speak of Galileo as "the Tuscan artist" who "through optic glass views [the moon's orb] at evening from the top of Fesole or in Valdarno, to descry new lands, rivers or mountains in her spotty globe." Milton molded new images and figures of speech from the material newly acquired through cognitive science. He had always kept abreast of contemporary natural philosophy and was thoroughly informed of the latest in scientific knowledge.

The French Revolution, essentially bourgeois in character, had blasted not only the Bastile, but also the bastions of Feudalism. Along with it the Revolution gave birth to a new class of people, the proletariat, the residual human byproduct of capitalist exploitation. Since then, capitalism has waged relentless wars against their victims, Nature and the Working Class. The poets and the intellectuals of eighteenth and nineteenth centuries were ambivalent in their attitude to these and there was no unanimity in their attitudes.

Among the eighteenth-century poets, Oliver Goldsmith (1728-1774) was very sensitive to the changes in Nature caused by capitalism, the nascent economic order. Realistically, he described the painful changes in the country-side in his poem "The Deserted Village". The village is deserted because, far away, in the city, there is rabid industrialization. The new urban surrounding was drawing men and women into its slums. Goldsmith discerns the menacing presence of a tyrant in the village who devastates the rustic scenes of simplicity:

> Ill fares the land, to hastening ills a prey
> Where wealth accumulates, and men decay....
> But times are altered; trade's unfeeling train
> Usurp the land and dispossess the swain.....

These very powerful lines contain Goldsmith's criticism of the agents of capitalism who, like tyrants, "usurp and dispossess" the masses and rob "the neighboring fields of half their growth." He describes the process of bourgeois exploitation which causes hazardous changes to man and his surroundings. The deserted village is the new environment, the victim of capitalist vandalism.

Poets like William Cowper (1731-1800), William Blake (1757-1827) and Thomas Gray (1716-1771), the precursors to Romanticism, were highly sensitive to the destructive changes that industrial urbanization had brought upon the rural scenes. Though not so passionate like Blake, William Cowper was acutely aware of the hazardous effects of the large-scale felling of trees for augmenting industrial production. William Blake felt very deeply the inestimable spiritual loss that industrialization was causing to human life. Perhaps, he was one of the first of English poets to note the qualitative change in human character that industrial capitalism was bringing about. Inspired only by cut-throat competition, capitalism had only one goal, profit, which poisoned every fiber of the human self. Blake condemned the dehumanizing impact of the economic life which destroyed the gardens of love and the innocent heavens of childhood. His *Songs of Innocence* and *Songs of Experience* are not mere comparisons of human childhood and adulthood. They are also comparative poetic studies of the pre-industrial and the industrial stages of social development and their natural consequences. Innate human innocence is corrupted by the aggressive competition in economic production. Blake found a chapel and a graveyard full of tombstones where once stayed his garden of love. So he wanted to build a Jerusalem, an ideal world of happy life and heavenly love in England's green and pleasant land.

More than any other pre-romantic poet, Robert Southey (1774-1843) had specific clarity about the political agents behind the wide-spread devastation of Nature that the new economic order was causing. He notes that European nations were responsible for wide-spread destruction of Nature. With equal insensitivity they were murdering innocent women and felling down trees and forests. Southey's sonnets on slave trade passionately denounce the resurgence of the evil of slavery in modern times due to colonial imperialism. Southey's use of the word 'waste', which was to gain greater currency later in Environment literature, is very significant. In his "After Blenheim" Old Kaspar tells his two grand children, Peterkin and Wilhelmine how, for riches, the English and the French had wasted the country-side:

> With fire and sword the country round
> Was wasted far and wide
> And many a childing mother then
> And new-born baby died...

Blake's vision of a Jerusalem in England was shared by the later romantic poets in various ways. Inherent in the idea of Jerusalem or Xanadu or similar utopia are the criticism of contemporary social system and the visions of political alternatives. In "Kubla Khan" S.T.Coleridge (1772 - 1834) invokes the magical enchantment of poetry to create an ideal pleasure dome in language. It is an escape, a flight away from reality, to a world of fantasy where visions are easily realized. Practically, it is the admission of the failure to transform social reality. Whether their imaginative escapades are ethically right or not, one thing is certain that they were hyper-critical of the political economy of capitalism. The effort of Coleridge and Southey to create the ideal social order of Pantisocracy on the banks of the Susquehanna River in Pennsylvania might be criticized as a romantic misadventure, but it was an implicit negation of the exploitative social system that dehumanized Man and denatured Nature.

The industrial capitalist has no respect either for Man or Nature. He exploits the resources of nature and the labor power of the worker for the production of goods for market consumption. Various recent natural calamities and climatic changes like global warming, rising sea level, landslides, storms and tempests indicate that Nature will not be always tolerant, but will retaliate vengefully. Coleridge had allegorically prophesied this in his "The Rime of the Ancient Mariner". The Ancient Mariner is a representative of modern man who insensitively causes injury to the beauty of Nature and to its beautiful creatures. The Mariner had killed an Albatross, the benevolent spirit of Nature. The reward of sin is death. But in this case it was more than death. The Mariner had to live through a life-in death, a series of unnatural experiences, excruciatingly bewildering and agonizing. All natural phenomena turned against him. All elemental forces of Nature - the sea, the sun, the air and the water - were inimical and they inflicted physical torture and spiritual agony on his body and soul. Coleridge's poetic warning, given in terms of the supernatural, is overtly moralistic.

William Wordsworth (1770-1850) and S.T.Coleridge, youthful and passionate supporters of the French Revolution, had turned renegades when they had to confront the harsh realities of the time. They renounced all that the Revolution had stood for and sought refuge in misty spiritualism and supernaturalism. It was a futile exercise in language, poetic and philosophic, to realize an essentially subjective ideal. Their romantic 'return' to Nature was, in essence, an unromantic or un-heroic 'turning away' from the realistic. Their nostalgic love of the past, the glorification of childhood, transcendental idealism and pantheistic super- naturalism were indirect reactions to the corruption in social life and Nature. In their major poems, they do not provide any direct realistic idea of the social forces at work; instead, they strive to inscribe social consciousness with a self-complacent subjective philosophy which has no roots in reality. They were unhappy poets, as W.H. Auden said about his contemporaries, who fled in horror from all problems to islands in their private seas where their thoughts, like castaways, found ease in endless petting. ('A Communist to Others', 140-143)

But more than any other English poet Lord Byron (1788-1824) had a surer and more realistic idea of the economic goings-on in England. He was actively involved in the practical politics of his day and used both his poems and Parliamentary speeches to champion the cause of the working class. Therefore, without seeking refuge in any philosophical self-deception, he fought for the Luddites, the machine wreckers, and other workers.

The plunder of natural resources and human surroundings had reached an unprecedented all time high in nineteenth-century. The developments in science and technology were hastening the speed and acceleration of all-pervasive change. Darwinian theories of Natural Evolution, Marxian theories of Dialectical and Historical Materialism and Surplus Value, and Freudian theories of Psychoanalysis provided spectroscopic insights into all aspects of life-Nature, Society and the Mind of Man. The over-all situation was one of progress and development in England though its imperial arms were casting pain and poverty in far away colonies as in India. Poets like Alfred Tennyson (1809-1892) had conformed to the situation and, like his Ulysses, he wanted to follow knowledge like a sinking star to the utmost bound of the horizon. But Matthew Arnold (1822-1888) was more concerned about the cultural impact of the democratic changes in the industrial age. Full of doubt and skepticism, he sought in Nature a reassurance for his Faith, and in poetry he found a compensation for the philistine culture.

During the eventful years of the 20th century, British poets like W.B. Yeats (1865-1939), W.H. Auden (1907-1973), T.S. Eliot (1888-1965), Stephen Spender (1909-1995), Louis Mac Niece (1907-1963), Dylan Thomas (1914-1953) and the War poets responded differently to the extensive damages done to nature by man. They vary from conservative religiosity to revolutionary extremism. In his poem "Coole and Ballylee, 1931", W.B.Yeats summed up his position:

> We were the last romantics—chose for theme
> Traditional sanctity and loveliness;....
> But all is changed, that high horse riderless,
> Though mounted in that saddle Homer rode
> Where the swan drifts upon a darkening flood.

He was acutely sensitive to the overwhelming changes which were disastrously transforming the structure of the world. So he depicted the wide-spread sense of anarchy in highly evocative symbols and images:

> Turning and turning in the widening gyre
> The falcon cannot hear the falconer;
> Things fall apart; the centre cannot hold;
> Mere anarchy is loosed upon the world,
> The blood-dimmed tide is loosed, and everywhere
> The ceremony of innocence is drowned;
> The best lack all conviction, while the worst
> Are full of passionate intensity.
> ("The Second Coming")

Some of these poets were ambivalent in their attitude to machines of war and war industry. Stephen Spender *did* praise the beauty of the train when it left the town:

> Beyond the town lies the open country
> Where, gathering speed, she acquires mystery,
> The luminous self-possession of ships on ocean.
> ("Express", 8-10)

But he struck another note when the air-passengers woke up to the sights of the town

> .....chimneys like black fingers

Or figures frightening and mad: and squat buildings
With their strange air behind the trees, like women's
faces
Shattered by grief.

> ("The Landscape near an Aerodrome", 16-19)

The dents that the natural phenomena leave on Auden's poetic imagination are unique. Unlike the romantic poets, Auden considered Nature purely for the moral and psychological anchoring that it could provide. In the poem "The Fall of Rome", Auden finds

Agents of Fisc pursue
Absconding tax-defaulters through
The sewers of provincial towns.

The contrast between the hopes of Thetis and her experience of reality in Auden's "The Shield of Achilles" brings out sharply the contrast between the world of vines, olive trees and untamed seas and the artificial wilderness and the sky like lead. The shield is not a thing of beauty, but a depiction of the harsh reality of the world, like the poem itself. The "thin lipped Hephaestus" is the artist, the poetic alter ego of Auden himself, who can depict only reality on the shield or in the poem:

A plain without a feature, bare and brown,
No blade of grass, no sign of neighborhood,
Nothing to eat and nowhere to sit down,
Yet, congregated on its blankness, stood
An unintelligible multitude,
A million eyes, a million boots in line,
Without expression, waiting for a sign.

T.S. Eliot's image of 'the waste land' sufficiently connotes without any shade of romantic sentimentality the destructive changes of modern times. The 'wasted' condition of the country-side, which Southey had noted at Blenheim, becomes universal in Eliot's world, "The Waste Land". Over a period of two and a half centuries, the land, the sea, the river, the city, the country and the street got so much transformed that everywhere one could see signs of decay and devastation. All places of human habitation are littered with "empty bottles, sandwich papers, silk handkerchiefs, cardboard boxes, cigarette ends" ("Waste Land", 177-178). At a time when "the human engine waits like a taxi throbbing waiting" it is not surprising

> The river sweats
> Oil and tar
> The barges drift
> With the turning tide
> Red sails
> Wide
> To leeward, swing on the heavy spar.
>
> ("Waste Land", 266-272)

The river in Eliot's "Dry salvages" (included in *Burnt Norton*) flows carrying the ravages of trade and commerce. The river is with "its cargo of dead negroes, cows and chicken coops" "a conveyer of commerce", and is "unhonored, unpropitiated by worshippers of machines." T.S.Eliot's "The Waste Land" is a masterpiece of environmental poetry. Quite intellectually and imaginatively, it deals with the after effects of extreme over-industrialization and commercialization in modern life. But the greatness of his insight is that he sees beyond the manifest physical changes and spots the consequent moral and spiritual degeneration.

The four centuries of English poetry provides an un-erasable chronicle of the changes that bourgeois forms of production have brought about in human social and natural environment. The major poems of great poets dialectically inscribe the impact of environmental changes on human sensibility and consciousness. English poets have reflected on the character of human activities on Nature as soon as capitalism took center stage of economic activity. In sensitively imaginative terms they have expressed their anxious misgivings about the extensive destruction of nature and the erosion of moral values in the wake of aggressive capitalistic greed. Using science and technology it mastered nature and redefined social and political equations. Though English poets are ambivalent in their attitude to the working class, there is unanimity in their concern for the devastation that over-industrialization and over-urbanization were causing to human environment. English poetry has been thematically evolving to an eco-political focus though its criticism of the conservative capitalistic development paradigm is not very much vocal.

ENDNOTES

1   Marlowe's Tamburlaine the Great is not a tyrant, but one who scans Nature with the eyes of a great adventurer

2   In his "Introduction" to the edition of *The Tempest,* Frank Kermode has quoted from Theodore Spencer's discussion of

the play. (Frank Kermode, "Introduction", *The Tempest,* 1954; rpt. London: Routledge, 1988, lxxxvii) Spencer considers the play as a study of the difference between appearance and reality. Also he considers it, "in terms of three levels in Nature's hierarchy -the animal, the human and the intellectual-which were the bases of Shakespeare's views of man". The 'intellectual', typified by Prospero, is the highest level in the Shakespearian hierarchy as he possesses ethical knowledge of Nature (and all our knowledge is of and about Nature) to define and design it for tomorrow.

MATTHEW ARNOLD:

THE VOICE AND THE VICTIM
OF BOURGEOIS CULTURE

The impact of Matthew Arnold who is usually termed as "the most imposing figure in English in mid-Victorian criticism" can be gauged from the general acceptance and the wide currency that his catchy phrases had during the early decades of the twentieth-century[1]. Terms like "disinterestedness", "high seriousness", "sweetness and delight", "Hebraism and Hellenism", "touchstone method", "liquidity of diction", "fluidity of movement" "architectonics", etc. were treated as the sure yardsticks for the critical assessment of literary works. But, later, there developed a sense of imperfection and inadequacy about his principles and practice of criticism. Wimsatt and Brooks have noted "some wavering, some slithering of logic" in Arnold. They refer to E. K. Brown who found Arnold's whole career "a tension between the impulse of detachment and that of practical application..." Both T. S. Eliot and F.R. Leavis have also expressed their discontentment with the critic in Arnold. More recently, Bernard Bergonzi has incidentally observed that Arnold's attitude to the development of English literatures in Canada and America as "supercilious".[2]

The words which Bergonzi selects for characterizing Arnold's attitude are "patronizing", "rhetoric", "international", "imperial", etc. They are all suggestive of the ideological power charges latent in the critical tools of Arnold which compelled him to take resort to abstractions. The bourgeois ideology, which Arnold enunciated with verve and vigor in his social and literary criticism, becomes a highly pronounced presence when we retrospectively reconsider it from the vantage point of modern studies on ideology.

Historical materialism alone answers comprehensively why human knowledge of natural, social and economic processes could come of age only in the nineteenth century. Ideology became a special intellectual concern when Marx and Engels threw self-reflexive light on it with their combined work *The German Ideology*. They used the term "ideology" pejoratively because German idealist philosophy, instead of explaining social reality, created false consciousness and kept people divided and deluded[3]. Subsequent to their critique of ideology, there have been numerous theoretical pursuits which underscored its role in social and mental structures[4]. Later Marxist thinkers like Antonio Gramsci, Louis Althusser, Walter Benjamin, Pierre Macherry, Raymond Williams and Terry Eagleton have explored the social meaning of ideology further. Discussing the concept of hegemony, Gramsci has maintained that ideology is materialistic in essence and every member of the human society is inescapably immersed in it, whether he likes it or not. Ideology is a field of class conflict and only ideological dominance can bestow a class with hegemonic importance.[5] According to Althusser, ideology represents the imaginary relationship of individuals to social reality.

All practice takes place in society in such a way that "ideology interpellates individuals" as its subjects[6]. The ideas of Gramsci and Althusser, introduced to English thought through Bakhtinian logic by Terry Eagleton, notes that the professed neutrality of artists and critics, in effect, extend unwitting support to the dominant ideology[7].

In nineteenth-century, the middle class had hegemonic importance in English society. The rapid spread of industry, trade, commerce and colonialism saw political hegemony passing from the landed aristocracy to the rising bourgeoisie. But, as it was historically inevitable, there arose its greatest challenge in the form of working class democracy. Bourgeois economic practice was hostile to the interests of the vast masses of common people. Kept unemployed and impecunious, they crowded the labor market. But for their sweat and blood, the bourgeoisie would not have attained economic progress and social power. However, though they had great sway on all economic and political matters, they could not boast of a culture that the aristocracy was proud of displaying. The situation had irreconcilable contradictions in it. The middle class, despite its economic supremacy, found its own deficiency when the cultural equation was drawn. The tension of the middle class to come to terms with the internal conflicts and contradictions of the socio-economic situation permeates all aspects of Matthew Arnold's poetry and criticism.

In this respect, young Matthew's tutelage under his formidable father Dr.Thomas Arnold was a formative ideological conditioner. The poem, *Sohrab* and *Rustom,* an expression of the "unconscious imaginative projection of the conflict" between a father and the son, has no biographical validation.[8] The poet-son adored his teacher- father. He had imbibed much of his father's religious faith and moral discipline. There is no biographical ground for any ideological conflict between the two. Then what is the source of the apparent conflict between the father and the son of the poem? In fact, the conflict is to be found in the two qualitatively different social realities that they were destined to mediate morally. Dr.Arnold stuck to the conventional religious morality of an earlier generation with more self-assurance, whereas his son found it rather difficult to do so as his world was more violently shaken by the cultural ethos of industrial capitalism. Arnold could not but respond to the impalpable and invidious demands of the middle-class (bourgeois) ideology. While resisting it, he had to allow himself to be tamed by it.

Arnold's denigration of the three classes in *Culture and Anarchy* (1869) as the Barbarians, the Philistines and the Populace, based on their responsiveness to the problems of culture, is replete with bourgeois bias. In a confessional manner he speaks out:

> Almost all my attention has naturally been concentrated on my own class, the middle class, with whom I am in closest sympathy, and which has been, besides, the great power of our day, and has had its praises sung by all speakers and newspapers.[9]

Arnold is conscious of the indebtedness of the other classes to the aristocratic class for the model it set. He cherishes its "vigor", "high spirit", "choice manners", "distinguished bearing", "good looks" "accomplishments" and "prowess". He would have given the aristocrats full marks had they "a shade more *soul*". Similarly, Arnold is hopeful that from among the working class a section might emerge who would sit "on thrones with commercial members of Parliament and other middle-class potentates". Arnold thinks that they might join the Philistines. It is the residual sections of the working class which Arnold calls the Populace. They are not exalted or edified and they are always rejected or pushed aside. They unsettle the "tranquil" life of the middle-class. While the Philistine triumphantly marches forward with one arm on the shoulders of the aristocrat and the other on that of the select section from the working-class, his smugness is mercilessly punctured into perplexities by the "vast residuum" who think they can assert "an Englishman's heaven-born privilege *of* doing as he likes" "by marching where it likes, meeting where it likes, bawling what it likes, breaking what it likes." Thus the economic and political dilemma of the middle-class gets transformed into tension and anxiety about the cultural anarchy issuing forth from "the Populace".

'The Function of Criticism at the Present Time', often acclaimed as Arnold's manifesto as a critic, begins by striving to resolve the dichotomy between poetry and criticism as to which is more important. Arnold notes that, unlike in other European languages, criticism does not find a prominent place in English. Assigning superiority to creative activity, he maintains that the source of "true happiness" is "not at all epochs and under all conditions possible."[10] The creative genius gets inspired by "the intellectual and spiritual atmosphere" of ideas, and "divinely" deals with them "in the most effective and attractive combinations". Arnold thinks in the vein of Taine to whom the synthesis of the man and the moment alone produced great works.

Arnold states that ideas, which are the elements of literature, are more within the control of the critical power. They create "an intellectual situation" to be profitably used by the creative power. Arnold views the relationship between a critic and a poet as that of a John to a Jesus.[11] The critic gives currency to the best ideas in society, implicitly preparing the way for the poet, the prophet.[12]

Arnold's view of critics as the source of great ideas is metaphysical or ideas can never be *suo generis*. Though he admits that they should have human sources, he confines them to specific persons designated as critics who are also entrusted with the task of their circulation. But the question is whether the critics, star-crossed to follow the profession of criticism, alone are the sources of ideas. And, if at all they are the fountainheads of great ideas, are they the only people interested in ideas? Are there not priests and politicians, concerned with great ideas, who can be treated as critics as well? Ambiguous in his parameters, Arnold cannot ascribe it to the complex social processes which involve all members directly or indirectly. He does not recognize and register the seminal importance they deserve as the never drying sources of ideas.

Arnold considers the qualitative difference in the poetry of Byron and Goethe to be the result of the qualitative difference in their interest in ideas. Arnold brands English romantic poetry as "premature" because of the absence of great ideas to work with. He portrays Byron as "empty of matter" and Shelley as "incoherent".

But he regrets that his favorite poet Wordsworth has to be grouped with them. Indulging in abstractions, he attributes the reasons for Wordsworth's disqualification to the lack of "completeness and variety" and to the absence of acquaintance with great authors like Goethe.

According to Arnold, Shakespeare could write great poetry because he lived during the Renaissance, the period of great intellectual movement. But, unlike Shakespeare, the English romantic poets were carried away by the passions of the French Revolution. The Revolution did not reach its natural culmination because it "took a political, practical character" half way and threw culture back. Arnold's criticism of the French Revolution reveals his limitation as a middle-class intellectual. He thinks that whereas the English Revolution was concerned with the legal, the French Revolution was concerned with the rational. When Arnold makes comparisons between the two, the contradiction in his approach becomes all the more evident. He admits that the French Revolution was "a more spiritual event than our Revolution" and that it had taken a more successful course practically. If we go by his own precept, we would see that the French Revolution did not produce any great poetry and that the English Revolution should not have produced any great poetry for the simple reason that it had taken a "successful" practical turn. But we do know that the English Revolution produced at least a great poet. John Milton, "the greatest English revolutionary who is also a poet, the greatest English poet who is also a revolutionary", was indeed the product of his time.[13] But as he could not admit to himself that any political idea or movement can produce great poetry, Arnold could not attribute Milton's greatness to the intellectual movement behind the English Revolution though he himself had maintained that "for the creation of a masterwork of literature two powers must concur, the power of the man and the power of the moment, and the man is not enough without the moment"[14]. To escape from this prison-house of self-begotten precept, Arnold has only one alternative which betrays the contradiction in him. In his essay on "Milton", included in *Essays in Criticism,* Arnold writes, "Nature formed Milton to be a poet".[15]

Arnold continues to maintain that French Revolution produced "an epoch of concentration" whose chief voice was Edmund Burke. The only sensible reason for Arnold's disapproval of the ways of the French Revolution is that it went against the politics of the class to which he belonged. The French Revolution, despite its leadership's bourgeois character, had raised hopes of an egalitarian society. And the English poets, like Byron and Shelley, had looked forward to a social structure without the inhuman exploitation of man by man?"[16]

How could Arnold with self-confessed sympathies for the middle-class, his own class, approve of a politics that undermined its very foundations? In this context anarchy was not only cultural disorder, but also social disarray with irrepressible political and economic repercussions. Therefore, Arnold's advocacy that "the English must modify their attitude towards public authority" is an indirect appeal to conform to the socio-political requirements of the middle-class[17].

The leaders like Danton had tried to give French Revolution a practical political turn. Their aim was to give the under-privileged masses their rightful place in history and in society. But the upper classes always plotted to turn the tides of the Revolution only "to the profit of landowners, of lawyers and tricksters"[18]. During the Revolution, the bourgeoisie had indeed appropriated many rights from the aristocracy with the help of the *canaille* or the proletariat. But when it came to the sharing of rights, the bourgeoisie handed over power to Napoleon, the capitalistic emperor of modern times. But the Napoleonic Code fell heavily on the workers banning their trade union rights and fell lightly on the bourgeoisie because it "was made by the bourgeoisie for the bourgeoisie; it was made by the owners of property for the protection of property"[19]. Therefore, the continuation of the Revolution to its logical conclusion of a socialistic society was an anathema not only to the French middle-class, but also to their brothers in England who were conscious of their newly acquired economic supremacy and political authority. They knew that self-sacrifice could be self-destructive. The contradiction in Arnold's criticism of the French Revolution lays bare the contradictions in his middle-class character.

As Arnold is not scientific or materialistic in his social criticism, he does not recognize the historical connection between the English and the French revolutions. On the other hand, Frederick Engels has made the following observation:"The English Revolution of the seventeenth century is nothing other than the prototype of the French Revolution of 1789...Cromwell is Robespierre and Napoleon in one..."[20] Analyzing the English character, Engels has noted that the middle-class English character is a contradictory mixture of

German and French elements.[21] The awareness of this contradiction, cited as a "self-releasing energy", is the source of "the Englishman's tremendous practical activity". But the incapacity to resolve the contradiction has impelled English philosophy to "empiricism and skepticism". Most philosophers and poets of the period, including Thomas Carlyle and Alfred Tennyson, were empirical and skeptic. In Arnold this contradiction is more marked than in others. The special esteem that Arnold had for Goethe, the supreme voice of the Iron Age, points to his preference to German philosophy. The source of Arnold's skepticism is his spiritual struggle against the materialistic advancements of science and technology. The empirical trait in his nature is evident from the "touchstone method", the critical practice that was a failure in theory and practice.

Arnold's chief complaint against the French Revolution is that in "quitting the intellectual sphere", it ran "furiously into the political sphere."[22] Here, obviously, Arnold is at fault as he does not recognize the dialectical relationship between precept and practice. No revolutionary idea can confine itself to the cerebral realm forever. It will exercise its natural impact on social and historical processes. When Arnold was 22 years of age, Engels wrote in 1844, "Social revolution is the only true revolution, to which political and philosophical revolution must lead..."[23]. But Arnold does not historicize the processes of ideas as he is against their practical employment. He seeks refuge in Utopian abstractions like disinterestedness:

> Its business is, as I have said, simply to know
> the best that is known and thought in the world,

and by in its turn making this known, to create a
current of true and fresh ideas."[24].

Arnold forgets the important fact that the touchstone
of all ideas is social practice, but he tries to fence them
off from all social praxis. Inevitably, implicit in this
apolitical idealism is the approval of the internally
corrupt *status quo.* Arnold considered that it was the
prerogative of some critical intelligence like his own
to propagate the best ideas from Olympian heights.
Arnold sought a divorce between theory and practice,
idea and action. As he had never realized the dialectical
relationship between the two, he did not comprehend
that ideas are fertilized only in the ground reality of
human practice. Also, just as he did not recognize that
there could be good or bad ideas, he did not realize that
there could be good or bad practice.

Conditioned as he was by the dominant bourgeois
ideology, Arnold's criticism could not grapple with
the complex problems which the century's economic
culture inevitably generated. In itself an idea is devoid
of any value. But, admittedly, there is the problem
of ideas being subjugated to ulterior selfish motives
which might leave a person unaware of his own "ideal
imperfection". This is true with respect to the ideas
which are kept away from the practical world. It is
possible that the critic, who is the sole source of ideas
in the Arnoldian sense, may develop a delusive sense of
his own ideal perfection. The only solution to this is to
submit every idea to the test of practice, keeping both
idea and practice open to constant and simultaneous
criticism. As this does not figure in Arnold's concept of
ideas, wrongly he equates the word "disinterestedness"

with the Indian idea of detachment or *anasakthi.* In the Indian way of life, *anasakthi* is part of one's Dharma or duty or moral action. Quite unconcerned about personal peril or profit, a person should act. This is the philosophy of *Karma* or Action, enunciated in the *Bhagavat Gita*:

Karmanyevaadhikarasthemaphaleshukadachana.

(Thy duty is to act, not to think of the result) At the beginning of the Great Battle of *the Mahabharata,* the advice of Lord Krishna to Arjuna was that he should consider it his duty to fight Evil. That a person can be detached at the practical level and in political action has been established in modern times by Mahatma Gandhi. He did not think that the idea of Freedom should be always abstract. He took it to the common man because it belonged to him. He tried to realize it through political action. He consistently tested his ideas through practice. Whenever he found either of the two was morally deficient, Gandhi would readily review and revise them both, often baffling and exasperating his more "practical" and "intelligent" disciples.

What a writer *does not* say is as significant as what he *does* say. The seemingly empty spaces in between a writer's utterances may be inhabited by not too apparent semantic suggestions. The "Function of Criticism' contains many traces of the ideological repression of the real intentions of Arnold. The shades behind the abstractions and contradictions are ideologically charged constructs. Arnold's refusal to involve ideas in practical application makes him an unwitting collaborator to the whole bourgeois system. He does not realize that the forced divorce between idea and application will not do any good either to the critic he cherishes or to the poet he idealizes.

No writer is free from ideological interpellation because, as Gramsci has pointed out, we live in it. Arnold happened to live at a time when ideological struggle was as acute as economic and political struggles. But it was a time when the full implications of class conflict in ideological formations like literature or criticism remained undetected. Even those who had studied the dimensions and dynamics of class conflict in other spheres of life did not scan how class conflict affected the ideological processes in the social system. It was not sinful of Arnold that he happened to be ideologically conditioned by the middle-class, the most influential social segment of his time. As Arnold lived in an ideologically premature age, his concepts of poetry, literature, criticism, culture, etc. were uncritical and they tended to concretize the ideological state apparatus. As he does not move out of the dominant ideology through criticism and self-criticism, Arnold wanders into abstractions and romantic mystifications. The function of Arnold's criticism, resultantly, is an ideological intonation of the cultural life of the Philistines to make it more malleable.

ENDNOTES

1   William K. Wimsatt and Cleanth Brooks, *Literary Criticism: A Short History* (Calcutta: Oxford and I B H, 1967) 436.

2   Bernard Bergonzi, *Exploding English: Criticism, Theory, Culture* (Oxford: Clarendon Press, 1990) 73-74.

3   Karl Marx and Friedrich Engels, *The German Ideology* (Moscow: Progress Publishers, 1976) 29-36

4   Raymond Williams, *Key Words: A Vocabulary of Culture and Society* (Glasgow: Fontana, 1976) 126-30.

5   Antonio Gramsci, *Selections from the Prison Notebooks: Antonio Gramsci*, ed. & tr. Quintin Hoare and Geffrey Nowell Smith (New York: International Publishers, 1971) 127-30

6   Louis Althusser, *Lenin and Philosophy and Other Essays. tr.* Ben Brewter (New York: Monthly Review Press, 1971) 127-86.

7   Terry Eagleton, *Ideology: An Introduction* (London : Verso, 1991) 222-24

8   J.D.Jump, *"Matthew Arnold". From Dickens to Hardy* (1958; rpt. London : Penguin Books, 1970) 309-23.

9   Matthew Arnold, "Culture and Anarchy" *Selections from Matthew Arnold,* ed. Miriam Allott (London : J M Dent & Sons, 1978) 217

10 Matthew Arnold, "The Function of Criticism at the Present Time", *The Critical Tradition* Vol.2 ed. S.Ramaswami and V.S.Seturaman (Madras: Macmillan, 1978) 17-43. All quotations from "The Function of Criticism" are from this edition.

11 Scott James, *The Making of Literature* (London: Mercury Books, 1963) 275.

12 These quotes are from *English Critical Tradition,* 19-23.

13 Christopher Hill, *Milton and the English Revolution* (London: Faber and Faber, 1977) 4.

14 *English Critical Tradition,* 20.

15 Matthew Arnold, "Milton", *Essays in Criticism,* second series, (London: St. Martin's Press, 1966) 38.

16 Leo Huberman. *Man's Worldly Goods,* 1946; rpt. (New Delhi: People's Publishing House, 1981) 183-203.

17 Jump, *From Dickens to Hardy,* 321.

18 Huberman, *Man's Worldly Goods* 157.

19 Leo Huberman. 158.

20 Karl Marx and Frederick Engels, "The Condition of England",
    Articles on Britain (Moscow: Progress Publishers, 1975) 13.
21 Article on Britain, 14-15.
22 Arnold, "The Function of Criticism at the Present Time",
    Selected Poems and Prose, ed. Miriam Allott, 196.
23 Article on Britain, 9.
24 Miriam Allott, 198.

THE DIALECTICS OF INTERPRETATION:

ASPECTS OF LINGUISTIC AND SEMANTIC CONVERGENCES

There is much complexity in the way in which Linguistics, Semantics and Hermeneutics operate and act upon each other and contribute to the understanding of diverse texts of communication. On reviewing western hermeneutics historically, we discern that certain formative tendencies have radically affected the whole gamut of interpretation. One of these is the progressive secularization and democratization of the hermeneutic process itself. Though the history of hermeneutics is traceable to the ancient Greek masters of thought like Socrates, Plato and Aristotle, it became a fervent social practice only when the Jewish rabbis and the Christian priests adopted specific methodologies for Talmudic and Biblical interpretations. With the disintegration of Feudal Europe, the Peasants' Revolts, the Protestant Reformation and nascent industrialization, there was a great democratic shift in all walks of life. It became manifest in the hermeneutic process when individual Christians claimed for themselves the right and authority for Biblical interpretation. They began to read and understand the Scriptures in their own divine light and asserted their spiritual right to seek communion with God without the shady mediation of priestly heads and their gray wisdom. Viewed in this way, John Milton's epics, *Paradise Lost* and *Paradise Regained*, stand out as classic examples of the interpretations on the Bible.

Not surprisingly, Germany, the venue of Lutheran Protestant Revolution against Papal authority, turned out to be the center of modern systematic and secular hermeneutics. Though Friedrich Daniel Ernst Schleiermacher (1768-1834), Martin Heidegger (1889-1976) and Hans Georg Gadamer (1900-2002) gave new insights into the nature of interpretation, the symptoms of shift from the languages of divine texts to the languages of human texts could be detected even earlier in the theories of Johann August Ernesti (1707-1781). He noted specially that the meaning of words was dependent on linguistic usage; that linguistic interpretation should be complemented by authorial psychology and individuality; and that interpretation should demonstrate a detailed knowledge of the contexts of the text, historical and geographical.

Following Ernesti, Johann Gottfried Herder (1744-1803) based hermeneutics on a sound philosophy of language. He wanted interpretation to determine linguistic usages and their meanings. As meanings are word usages, an interpreter must explore the author's language and imaginatively recapture its meaning. He considered an individual's thought to be dependent on his capacity for linguistic expression. He complemented the importance given to language with an equal insistence on authorial psychology. Also Herder considered the role of *genre* in interpreting not only the linguistic texts but also the non-linguistic art. He valued interpretation for its central role in the disciplines of history, politics and culture and considered it essential in the promotion of inter-cultural understanding. Schleiermacher's hermeneutic views were grounded on a philosophy of language that exalted it to the range of a universal discipline. According to him, meaning consisted in "the unity of word-sphere" and an interpreter should understand an author. Introducing several forms of semantic holism, he suggested that linguistic interpretation should be complemented with psychological penetration.

Manifest in the views of these philosophers is the importance of linguistics in interpretation. They almost treated it, along with meaning (semantic aspects), to be the essential constituents of the hermeneutical process. They shared and handed down to their successors the view that meaning and thought are dependent on language. Implicit in the views of Ernesti, Herder and Schleiermacher is the notion of a dialogue between the author or the text and the reader, the interpreter. In Hegelian hermeneutic thought, the presence of the idea of a dialogic process is very much evident as he conceived all intellectual processes as evolving and taking shape through the progressive frame of thesis, anti-thesis and synthesis. Therefore, in his concept of meaning, the interpreter's task is not to recapture the original meaning of the author, but to relate the past meanings to one's own meanings and thoughts (to engage oneself in a dialogue with the past).

Though the relationship between language and meaning and their explication have been of great interest to the scholars of the East and the West, both ancient and modern, the structure and meaning of language becomes an object of special interest and interpretation in the modern West only with the New Critics. Salvaging rhetoric from the low depths into which it had fallen, I.A.Richards (1893-1979) noted that "most words, as they pass from context to context, change their meanings; and in many different ways".[1] He refused to admit the notion of the stability of the meaning of words: "Stability in a word's meaning is not something to be assumed, but something to be explained." Richards goes on to explain the connection between the language user's mind and the world, the problems involved in the gestation and generation of meaning. His enquiry into the essential aspects of literary language convinced him that 'ambiguity', generally considered a blemish in linguistic expressions, is a virtue, an essential attribute of its 'literariness'. Richards blasted the notion of the eternal sanctity of the meaning of linguistic expression: a word "utters not one meaning, but a movement among meanings". Following Richards, William Empson (1906-1984) took pains to explain how, through semantic ambiguities, literary language created the possibility for the clash and coalescence of meanings. Empson elucidated his views in his *Seven Types of Ambiguity* (1930) and *The Structures of Complex Words* (1951) and brought to bear upon language the historical and sociological contextuality of words by which he never meant "to simplify interpretation or to cut down ambiguity."[2]

More than the British and the American New Critics, the European structuralists were concerned with the perception and description of the structures of language and their semantic orientation. The traces of structuralism, found in *New Sciences* (1725) by Giambattista Vico (1668-1774), were developed by Jean Piaget (1896- 1980), the Swiss psychologist, and Ferdinand de Saussure (1839-1914), the Swiss linguist and Sanskrit scholar. According to Piaget, a structure embodies the ideas of wholeness, transformation and self-regulation. Saussure revolutionized linguistics with his semiotic ideas and exercised a great influence on Russian Formalists and French structuralists with his formative principles in *A Course in General Linguistics* (1916), a posthumous publication by his students as homage to their great master. To Saussure, language is an arbitrary structure of signs. A sign is anything that tells us about something other than itself. Saussure considered language a semiotic system based completely on opposition between its concrete units. To mean a system of language requires differences; it is differences that carry meanings. Saussurean structural semiology has, thus, become a byword for modern linguistics, the science of linguistic structure, and has, as a tendency of thought, cast great influence on other disciplines like Literary Theory, Literary Criticism, Anthropology, Mythology and Sociology.

In leading structural linguistics to more subtle ways and in applying it to literary semantics and interpretation, the contribution of Roman Jakobson (1896-1982), is of great importance. Jakobson developed the technique for the phonological, morphological and syntactical study of language. Drawing in intellectuals like Roland Barthes and Claude Levi-Strauss, he made Saussurean structural semiotics a major intellectual movement in modern times. His main contribution to linguistics is his model for the analysis of discourse which outlines the key constituents of communication and their related functions. But more than anything else his definition of the poetic function as "the projection of the principle of equivalence from the axis of selection to the axis of combination" is said to underscore the structural hallmark of poetry. It implies that poetry successfully combines and integrates form and function that turns the poetry of grammar into the grammar of poetry.

Though never monolithic in character, the Russian Formalist School had several prominent theorists who considered the formal "devices" employed in literary works "to make a semantic orientation". But, generally, the excessive emphasis that they laid on the formal aspects of the text prevented its fruitful interpretation. However, Viktor Shklovsky's idea of "defamiliarization" gets prominent consideration in the structuralist thoughts of the Czech linguist Jan Mukarovsky, one of the founders of the Prague Linguistic Circle. In "Standard Language and Poetic Language", he maintains that it is the aesthetically intentional distortion of the linguistic components which creates poetic sense and effect[3]. In poetry there takes place the systematic violation of the norm of the Standard Language; the poet foregrounds certain linguistic elements which deautomatize the scheme of the familiar language and draw the reader's attention to itself. A multiplicity of interrelationships, generated by select deviant uses of words, figures of speech, syntax, intonation, etc., creates a dialectical interface within the literary text whereby the poet achieves effective communication. Even those uses of language, which are erroneous by conventional standards, can create poetic sense from the conflict and tension that the linguistic context evokes. Examining the problem of the aesthetic along with his idea of art as sign and structure, Mukarovsky has maintained that aesthetic valuation has great importance in the refinement of language. Good language is that which helps "foreground" the aesthetic. Thus slang, dialect, foreign loan words, poetic neologisms, semantic jumps and breaks, etc. contribute to the foregrounding - to the unexpectedness, the unusualness, and the uniqueness - of the poetic language and the creation of aesthetic value.

The contribution of Roland Barthes was very significant in leading Saussurean semiotics beyond the borders of structuralism. Barthes was concerned with the correct use of words and he always wanted to distinguish between "nature" and "culture". To him social institutions, intellectual habits, language and literature were not natural phenomena, but arbitrary signs and social constructs. Words work in the way they do because of the place they have in the structure of language. Barthes was, initially, in agreement with Saussure's idea of semiotic arbitrariness and differences that played the role of semantic determinants in linguistic communication. But with his 1967 essay "the Death of the Author" he moved over to Jacques Derrida's ideas of Deconstruction and argued that the term "author" (*auteur*) should be rejected and replaced by that of "writer" (scripteur), somebody who writes. For Barthes, it is the reader who decides the meaning of a text.[4]

In *System de la Mode* (1967), through the semiotic interpretation of Fashion, Barthes showed how semiology worked in linguistics. He brought semiology into everyday life and considered it a sort of Sartrean "bad faith" not to make conscious choice of the signs with which we want to project our self-image onto the world. He shared with the Marxists a strong disapproval of the middleclass ways of life and views on literature. According to him, the bourgeois theories of art strive to convince the readers of the reality of what is read. They make them think that the signs are natural. This, in effect, is an implicit demand to accept the social class division as natural. Barthes considered literature as a way of exploiting linguistic signs for preserving cultural dominance. Through many examples he suggested that literary interpretation along semiotic lines would help understand class relations. He was of the view that many features of literature and language would be illuminated by the new researches in the field of linguistics, semiotics, psychoanalysis and Marxism[5].

The central idea running through the works of Barthes is that there is an element of intellectual imperialism inherent in language. It is fascistically compelling and cannot be altered, though it can be relentlessly questioned. That literature always calls its own language into question is its greatest virtue. Therefore, there can never be any final interpretation of a work of literature. Texts are always open and always subject to be re-written in the mind of the reader. A never ending dialogue takes place between the text and the reader and it helps the reader maintain his interpretative freedom. Literature is the proof and assertion of human freedom as interpretation is an insistent process of interrogation.

Though a shade of the politics of philosophy is discernable in Barthes's concept of "freedom through literature", during his Deconstructionist phase, as a literary theorist, Barthes granted almost anarchic interpretative freedom to the reader. Generally called Post-structuralism, Barthian Deconstruction considered every sign different from all other signs in endless ways. Unlike in Saussurean linguistics, in deconstructive thought, signs had no safe stay. The comfortable view, that between the "signifier" and the "signified" the sign was a symmetrical semantic unity, yielded place to "the spin-off of a potentially endless play of signifiers". In every sign, as there were present the shades and shadows of all other signs, meaning was inexhaustible and ever modifiable. The simple purity of the Saussurean sign was thus lost in the semantic fluidity and plurality of Deconstruction. The reader was free to exploit the rhetorical nature of language to any extreme limit. Derrida countered the phono-centric or logo-centric view of language, dominant in western philosophy ever since Plato, and maintained that all transcendental or metaphysical concepts of meanings were fictitious. He went against all conventional ideas of interpretation and indulged in over-interpretation, making the very purpose of hermeneutics meaningless. With his idea of "the rustles and ruptures of language," Derrida had erased the distinction between creative literature and philosophy. The Deconstructionists, generally, forgot the fact that language is not a self-created realm of itself. It is inalienably linked to the world and society, our day to day life. It is of what we do, by what we do and for what we do. The whole being of ours is a relentless process of change and transformation of which language is an agent. Life and language necessitate endless interpretation, perhaps, differing and deferring, but always moving and meaning.[6]

The deconstructionist semantic anarchy had its approvers and detractors. But also it had its critics who quickly realized the negative politics of Derrida's postmodernism and tried to erase his impact with the logic of Bakthinian dialogism. Relying on the linguistic and semantic aspects of neo-rhetoric, Dick Leith and George Meyerson have implied the idea of a dialogue involving a speaker (an addresser) and a listener (an addressee). According to them, "verbal interaction is the ultimate reality in language" which is part of the social world. The liberating revival of rhetoric provides for the diversification of analysis, the multiplication of meanings and the expansion of experience, which is the ultimate aim of all hermeneutic exercise[7].

Bakhtin's major works deal with the dialogic quality of language and the semiotic quality of discourse. He evolved a new science of language called Translinguistics and the Poetics of Utterance.[8] The object of translinguistics is discourse represented by utterance. Bakhtin was always opposed to the idea of the singularity of truth in the world as he had a mind that relished the plenitude and plurality of differences. He held a dialogue with the major movements of his time and emphasized the cognitive and the social in language. He discerned the structures of interpersonal relations in a "world in between consciousness" and invested such terms as 'dialogue' and 'utterance' with new meanings. Dialogue is not a conversation between two people, but "a communication" under "extensive set of conditions" "between simultaneous differences." To Bakhtin everything means. He was always pre-occupied with freedom. Like Barthes, who found liberty in the interrogative possibility of the literary language, Bakhtin grounded it "in the dialogic nature of language and society."

Unlike the Personalists (Wilhelm Wundt, Benedetto Croce) who claimed "I own meaning" and the Deconstructionists who declared "no one owns meaning", Bakhtin asserted "*we* own meaning". Bakhtin rooted meaning in the social, realized dialogically. Meaning is the product of dialectical interactions. The word is the territory shared by the speaker (addresser) and the listener (addressee).[9] Bakhtin's Dialogism provides a comprehensive linguistic philosophy that perceives all aspects of human life as originating in language. The abundant variety of life and its reality cannot be studied by one discipline alone. So he studied the role of signs in human thought and in linguistic utterance. He realized that society and history invested words with worlds and meanings. According to him, the word exists only in the dialogic context which belongs to history. Discourse is always inter-individual:

> Language acquires life and historically evolves precisely here, in concrete verbal communication, and not in the abstract linguistic system of language forms, nor in the individual psyche of speakers[10]

Differences in meaning can be registered only between two speakers. Always a word is targeted towards an addressee. Whereas grammar tends to systematize a language, linguistic contexts resist order and organization. Bakhtin writes: "…the word is a two-sided act. It is determined equally by whose word it is and for whom it is meant. A word, it is precisely the product of the reciprocal relationship between speaker and listener, addresser and addressee….A word is a bridge thrown between myself and another…it is a territory shared by both addresser and addressee."[11] He considered language as the stage where different social accents are voiced. It is the interaction of social forces that brings a word into being. Language is the product of the social milieu. Social life determines the nature and structure of an utterance. Unlike the structuralists, who extricated words from their social contexts, and unlike the Deconstructionists, who made interpretation interminable, Bakhtin maps the meaning of utterances in their social contexts. A speech is a discourse in action. All speech is rhetorical and, therefore, ideological and semiotic. Only in inter-individual territory a sign can *be and mean.* A word and an experience are made what they are by the meaning they hold and communicate. It is 'theme' which makes them distinct; and 'theme' is characterized by varying contexts. Bakhtin understands the dialectical relationship between theme and meaning, the two building blocks of utterance. A person who considers an utterance has to deal with the otherness of the whole situation. According to him, any true understanding is dialogic in nature and meaning is realized only in the process of active, responsive understanding. Meaning is, as Katerina Clarke and Michael Holquist state, "not in the word or in the soul of the speaker or in the soul of the listener. Meaning is the effect of interaction between speaker and listener produced via the material of a particular sound complex."[12]

Bakhtin's Dialogism convincingly rebuts the anarchy of interpretation unleashed by the post-structuralists led by Derrida under the influence of the hermeneutic ideas of Hans-Georg Gadamer. A text, religious or literary or non-literary, is a semiotic manifestation of an aspect of its author's consciousness. A reader or an interpreter who confronts it is likely to bring in his ideas while dealing with it. Naturally, there ensues a dialogue between the text, the structured consciousness of the author, and that of the interpreter. The thesis meets its antithesis and the resultant synthesis is the meaning, the interpretation. Neither the total negation of the authorial consciousness, nor the total domination of the interpreter's consciousness takes place. Dialogue moves on to another level. After meaning, it moves on to mean.

Shakespeare's plays were written more than four hundred years ago. Since then there have been numerous translations, stage adaptations and film versions of the great plays. Besides these, hundreds and thousands of scholars and critics have spent laborious days and nights reading, interpreting and criticizing them. Despite the innumerable new readings and interpretations, Shakespearean texts still hold sway in spite of the best efforts of all semantic anarchists to declare him dead. What is it that has kept Shakespeare unscathed all these years and has enabled him to carry on his dialogue with posterity? That the semiotic composition goes on engaging the readers with semantic resonances even now is an indication of the artistic success of Shakespeare's dramatic poetry, an assertion of the authority of his poetic consciousness. This is not the defeat of the reader, either. Together Shakespeare and his readers move on to another level of understanding.

Unconventional meanings can be read into religious icons, sometimes. The salutary example is Jesus Christ. Christians have been worshipping Christ for centuries. If there was unanimity of what Christ meant to them, surely, there would have been only one Christian Faith. By virtue of his martyrdom he is an ideal for political activists now and it is a new meaning read into the Christ myth. Christ, the sign, becomes a living voice when interpreted in this way.

Hermeneutics provides room for interminable dialogue. Interpretation is a dialectical process at the synchronic and diachronic levels. The interpreter dialogically engages not only the literary and non-literary texts, ancient and modern, but also his own historical past and present. Besides, the synchronous can engage the diachronous dialogically and reorient the meanings continuously through reinterpretation. Any dialogue with the past will resuscitate the meanings it holds for the present and the future, and, conversely, help re-examine the past in a new light. It will help reform the present and form the structures of the consciousness of the Future. Time present, in perpetual dialogue with time past, synthesizes the deferred future evolutionarily. All hermeneutic exercise is a prediction and predication of the dialogue between time present and time past. Interpretation is not a monologic, but a dialogic process:

> Time present and time past
> Are both perhaps present in future
> And time future contained in time past.[13]

ENDNOTES

1   I.A.Richards, *The Philosophy of Rhetoric*, (Oxford: Clarendon Press, 1989)11.

2   Jonathan Culler, *Framing of the Sign* (Oxford: Basil Blackwell, 1986) 85-95.

3   Jan Mukarovsky, *"Standard Language and Poetic Language", Linguistics and Literary Style,* ed. Donald C.Freeman (New York: Holt, Rinehart &Winston, 1970) 42-44.

4   Roland Barthes, "The Death of the Author", *Issues in Contemporary Critical Theory,* ed. Peter Barry (London: Macmillan) 53-55.

5   Roland Barthes, "Literature as Rhetoric", *Sociology of Literature and Drama: Selected Writings,* ed. Tom Burns and Elizabeth Burns (Harmondsworth: Penguin books, 1973) 191-197.

6   Jacques Derrida, *Of Grammatology* (Delhi: Motilal Banarasidas Publishers, 1994) 50.

7   Dick Leith and George Meyerson, *The Power of Address: Exploration in Rhetoric* (London: Routledge, 1989) 72.

8   Mikhail Bakhtin, "Dialogic Discourse", *The Bakhtin Reader: Selected Writings of Bakhtin, Medvedev and Volosinov,* ed. Pam Morris (London: Edward Arnold, 1994) 26-87.

9   Mikhail Bakhtin, *Marxism and Philosophy of Language,* trans. Ladislav Matejka and I.R.Titunik (New York: Seminar Press, 1973), 85-86.

10   Mikhail Bakhtin, *Bakhtin Reader, 59.*

11   Mikhail Bakhtin, *Marxism and Philosophy of Language,* 85-86.

12   Katerina Clarke and Michael Holquist, Mikhail Bakhtin (Cambridge: Harward U P, 1984) 232.

13   T.S.Eliot, "Burnt Norton", *Four Quartets,* Delhi: OUP, 1962.

BARTHES AND BAKTHIN:

MONOLOGIC AND
DIALOGIC SEARCHES FOR MEANING

Roland Barthes's search for the meaning of linguistic signs leads him to conclude that literature, as it constantly calls language into question, is the only proof and assertion of human freedom. With the cue from Ferdinand de Saussure, he has logically applied the principles of structuralist semiotics to the study of popular culture and has affirmed that every form of human social behavior employs its own sign systems, governed by their own rules. Always concerned with the distinction between nature and culture, Barthes does not consider the signs of language natural though they are arbitrary conventions like the signs of other social conventions, performances and practices. He has elaborated the Saussurean idea of the mutual difference of signs in structural contexts which generates meanings. In a syntagmatic context, according to him, no sign is natural. And where they seem to be the most natural, the most artificial they are. In the essays in *Mythologies* (1957), Barthes has re-emphasized the idea that the sign-signified relationship is arbitrary and that meaning is an artificial and motivated cultural construct.

However, in "The Death of the Author" (1967), Barthes has fought deconstructively against author-centeredness in literary criticism, as it is "the epitome and culmination of capitalist ideology which has attached great importance to the 'person' of the author" and has celebrated "the desacrilization of the image of the author."[1] As signs (words) evoke meanings from their semiotic differences, once the artefact (syntagmatic structure) comes into being, the writer has no authority in determining the final meaning of the text. Mercilessly, Barthes has pulled down the author from the high pedestal and has tried to bury him deep, unceremoniously. His argument is that simultaneous to "the death of the author" "the birth of the reader" occurs; every new reader marks the textual signs and maps their meanings in diverse cognitive contexts, giving room for new discoveries and new connotations; the text may have a single author, but its plentiful readers can exploit its semantic suggestiveness endlessly.

In his semiotic analysis of everyday life, Barthes has espoused the Marxian version of Sartrean existentialism that defined human freedom as the freedom of choice. The encoding of a message, therefore, involves the selection of appropriate codes for the message, an existential praxis that deliberates on the form and content of communication. The author's selection of signs from a paradigm and their syntagmatic placing are viewed as intentional and premeditated. As the communicator's motive indicates, authoring is not a disinterested endeavor. Nor is it a purposeless sign game without semantic orientation. So Barthes has considered every form of communication artificial, never reflecting the 'real' reality. He has questioned the traditional view which held language and literature real and natural. According to him, this is part of the historic social deception practiced by the bourgeois society which conveniently treats the conventions of language as natural. Barthes is convinced that the clarity of French prose is a bourgeois characteristic which should be broken by the motivated practice of *illisibilite* (unreadability), the opposite of clarity as a strategy for questioning.

Though, with the idea of intentionality, Barthes has modified Saussure's concept of arbitrariness, his "Death of the Author" is an intense argument for asserting the autonomy of the reader. As author-centered literary criticism implicitly ratifies the exploitative bourgeois social system and its concomitant idea of supernatural predetermination of class distinctions and privileges, he has attacked the mimetic theory of literary creation that claims to reflect reality. Relishing the plurality of meanings, Barthes has given prominence to the reader and has directed him to seek liberation in language. In "From Work to Text", Barthes has subtly differentiated the "Work" and the "Text"; the former, a collection of syntagmatic encoding; and the latter, a product of semantic decoding. He stated: "While the work is held in the hand, the text is held in language: it exists only as discourse"[2]. The "Work", as he has maintained here, is an authored, but unread, volume; the "Text" is the resultant of reading, an "irreducible plurality."[3] A text, in which and with which a reader can "write" new meanings is an ideal "writerly" text. But a text where the reader passively consumes pre-cooked meanings is a "readerly" one.

However, Barthes has not worked out the author-reader dichotomy in a dialectical manner. Instead, he proceeds to negate and nullify the authorial semiotic presence in the text: "The Text...is read without the father's signature...The Text can be read without its father's guarantee: the restitution of the intertext paradoxically abolishes the concept of filiation."[4] Here, in his enthusiasm to privilege the reader, Barthes ignores the socio-linguistic and socio-psychological components, the constituents of the author's consciousness.

According to Barthes, the ideal reader resists the fascism of language and will not allow any "enunciative subject" to preside over the dispensation of meaning. The lexical difference that helps saying and meaning something, also prevents something else from being stated or suggested. Barthes's conclusion is that literature gives room for eternal interpretation. As no final meaning is necessary and possible, the texts are always open and, resisting closure, they subject themselves to endless interpretations. The reader, ideally, questions the 'texted' language, engaging himself in an uninterrupted monologue, a unilateral interpretation of the codes. In Barthian reading, the patriarchal author suffers elimination as he is not treated as the signatory of the instruments of meaning. As it gives almost anarchic freedom to the reader, the reading process becomes an unending monologue and ends up as a reductive endeavor. It culminates in an impressionistic annexation of signs and their signifieds. Eventually, reading degenerates to a reactionary effort that deflects the signs from their projected targets, something that Barthes as a critic of the bourgeois system has always disapproved. As Barthes ignores the social and ideological factors which influence both the author and the reader and how they happen to be 'written into' and 'read from' the text, his line of argument inevitably ends up in a lopsided privileging of the reader. He seems to subscribe to the old pleasure principle of literature: "Text.... is linked to enjoyment (*jouissance*), to pleasure without separation."[5] In the world of Barthian semiotics, the reader trails the frills of anarchic interpretative freedom. Barthes has ignored the fact that the reader, like the author, is a product of the complex social and historical processes. He idealizes the reader who is "...without history, biography, psychology" and he "is simply that *someone* who holds together in a single field all the traces by which the written text is constituted"[6]

Though, by virtue of his personal creative faculty the author can distinguish himself from the other members of the society, he is also exposed to the positive and negative influences of ideologies like them. Whether he likes it or not, all sorts of ideologies will address the 'author-subject' in him and will get themselves inscribed into his consciousness. Social history, ridden with class conflicts, inscribes itself on the author's consciousness which, subsequently, leaves its indelible imprint on the signs. The class character of the signs in the composition, visible to a discerning eye in varying shades of intensity, has its source in the author's ideological position. Signs are the direct or indirect vehicles of class ideology. The author intentionally erects ideological sentry posts of signs to guard his message from anarchic readers and also to lead them to the heart of the matter, the experience embodied in the message. He has a rhetorical axe to grind!

Barthes's concept of the author was influenced by his opposition to the Feudal Patriarch and the post-Renaissance capitalist, the dispensers of money, meaning and power. Clearly, he struck a parallel between the author and the bourgeois, the owner of meaning and the custodian of capital, respectively. Desiring to clean the semiotic world of all authorial monopoly over meaning and, emulating Nietzsche, who pronounced the death of God, Barthes tried to conduct the funeral rites of the "Author-God" whose demise was thought to have taken place in the backyard of Deconstruction. It was almost an obsessive conviction with him that "… the birth of the reader must be at the cost of the death of the author."[7] A fact that Barthes ignored is that, in modern times, the author is no god. He is not a patriarch in the field of letters. The democratic composition of the society allows every individual to be an author, and simultaneously, it allows every other individual to be a reader. The reader and the writer change their persona according to changing contexts. A reader may be a writer in one context and vice versa. Readers and writers are members of the same society, sharing the same ideological complexities, but engaged in diverse rhetorical practices. The proliferation of different kinds of media allows ample freedom for all to transmit and receive signals. It is not from the exalted pedestal of the author-god alone that modern writers communicate. Democracy, despite its bourgeois limitations, provides ample space for multi-level dialogues. Besides, the democratic spread of literacy has made language and literature accessible to all; literacy and literature are no more elite luxuries. There are many who have something to speak or to write and there are many who want to hear the spoken or to read the written. No more a deity, the author is only one of the demos, a Whitman speaking to fraternal humans. The author is not a class antagonist to the reader. The modern author and the modern reader cohabit, cooperate and communicate as well as they confront and contradict mutually. In short, they exist and function dialectically. The modern reader is not a passive recipient framed in pre-fabricated semantic codes. He is an interested party in the process of dialogue. Through the mediation of the text and exploiting the umpteen dialogic possibilities open to them, the author and the reader engage each other in incessant, purposeful and targeted dialogue. There need not be any class antagonism or high-low dialogic voltage variation between them to make communication possible. On democratic plains, with mutual respect and a sense of camaraderie, they make fraternal dialogues possible. Staying together on the same side, they can engage themselves in dialogues for breaking social and class barriers. The author-reader dialectics can progress from the level of thesis-antithesis to a higher level of semantic synthesis.

It is Mikhail Bakhtin's literary theory that counter-weighs the unilateral or lopsided importance given to the reader in Barthian semiotics. Unlike Barthes, Bakhtin sets a great store by the social psychology of language and, very logically, examines the dynamics of ideology that automatically in-forms every sign during its syntagmatic gestation. The society and the individual breathe and live in ideologies and, naturally, according to him, every sign bears their stamp. Ideologies are subtly inscribed into the signs and, through them, into human consciousness. As the historical evolution of the society has resulted in class stratification, the diverse ideological formulations, which receive local habitation in signs, have their distinct class character. More often than never, the writer, who chooses signs for transmitting his message, is guided, consciously or unconsciously, by the invisible presence and force of ideology. The consciousness of every member of the society, including that of the writer and the reader, is formed through a historical process that has brought class stratifications into existence. Therefore, when ideologies pervade the signs and signs become the transmitters of human consciousness, the class character of the members of the society gets semiotic statement. The writer and the reader are not ideologically innocent. They have their class ideology and character rhetorically charged in the linguistic codes.

Though Barthes has touched upon the ideas of Saussure, Jakobson and Derrida, he does not develop any of them into a philosophy of language. Is he eclectic? Whatever, Barthes is a consistent critic of the middle-class bourgeois attitude which reinforces the idea that the available social order is natural as language and its meaning. Substantiating the findings about the arbitrariness and artificiality of language, he has critically submitted that the present class differences are not natural, but artificial and deserving of transformation. However, unwittingly perhaps, Barthes has equated the social structure with the linguistically structured text and vested the task of its semantic de-structuring with the reader. He does not view the meaning which emanates from the text as of any social consequence. Contrary to Barthes, Bakhtin has a philosophy of language, a unifying theory termed "translinguistics". The idea of "dialogue" as an informing principle in interpersonal relations is central to Bakhtin's philosophy of language which, in itself, is a part of his comprehensive dialectics of nature and society. Therefore, differing from the structuralists who sought the source of meaning in semiotic differences, Bakhtin considers all words as bearing the imprint of society and as capable of impacting upon it ideologically. The numerous ideologies, part of the plurality and fluidity of the society, get worked into linguistic signs, the words. Unlike the linguist, the user of a language adapts words to changing situations and creates new meanings to suit the new, but concrete, social situations. Whereas the linguist falls into the trap of form, the language user creates a meaningful novelty.

Bakhtin's life-long concern, as in the case of Barthes, has been with the nature of language and its everyday application. Bakhtin has always relished the plenitude of differences and the plurality of meanings arising out of the complex factors which make dialogues possible. Recognizing the social dynamics of dialogue, Bakhtin has worked it up into a comprehensive set of conditions where communication can take place inexhaustibly. Bakhtin's specific term for referring to the incidence of communication enacting differences in values is "utterance". Difference, to him, is not merely the Saussurean formal difference that gives room for meaning; but it is also a difference in values, with social base, semiotic form and ideological charge and temper.

The difference between Barthes and Bakhtin can be seen as an extension of the similarities between them.

Both value "freedom" as the supreme achievement of human consciousness. Barthes considers literature the only realm where the reader can experience absolute and untrammeled freedom. Master of interpretations, the Barthian reader relegates the author to the position of an unwelcome guest. The text can offer a free meal of meanings to him who relishes them, unmindful of the cook. But it is a fact of common experience that the reader, like a god, cannot make meanings out of semiotic nothingness; he is effective only in an inter-semiotic void. Barthes over-privileges the reader and gives him absolute and almost anarchic freedom for over-interpretation. The result of a partial vision, it unilaterally marginalizes the author and forces him to fade into comparative insignificance.

Subtly differing from Barthes, Bakhtin views everything in the light of his concept of "Dialogue". For him, therefore, the experience of freedom is not to be derived from the absence of the author. Nor is it a celebration of the death of the author. As Katerina Clarke and Michael Holquist note, "Liberty for him [Bakhtin] is grounded not in the will of a monologic God, the inevitable course of history, or the desire of man, but rather in the dialogic nature of language and society"[8]. Bakhtin's position is, thus, dialectically socio-linguistic. His dialogism guides him to move away from the Personalists' claim of monopoly in meaning and the Deconstructionists' assertion of semantic anarchy. He holds the view that meaning is neither the author's nor the reader's. Meaning is not owned by "I" or "You", but by "We", the dialectical union of the author and the reader. Meaning is the dialectical product of two social events-of writing and of reading. Meaning is 'of' the text, 'by' the text and 'for' the 'texted we'. The reader proceeds to the meaning, whatever, through the text, the literary signs. The author-reader dialectics produces meaning. To his voice the author gives meaning with the voice and the meaning of others. He speaks to, and with, the others. Meaning is the resultant of the dialogue between the authored text and the 'texted reader'. To Bakhtin, "the word was a two-sided act. It is determined equally by whose word it is and for whom it is meant…A word is territory shared by both addresser and addressee, by the speaker and his interlocutor."[9]

The idea of the possibility of infinite number of meanings is a tall deconstructionist claim. A literary sign is always loaded with the ideological consciousness of the speaker/writer. Ideology is the social terrain where the politics of economics and class works either visibly or invisibly, but always causing subterranean ideological turbulence. The text, an utterance, bears ideological inscriptions on the consciousness of the author who designs a dialogue with his possible readers. The author's ideological intentions, manifest or buried, address the reader rhetorically. The writer and the reader do not live in any ideological vacuum. They are, concurrently, agents and victims of socially active ideologies. With receptive ears and discerning eyes, the reader scans the utterance, the text. He becomes a 'texted' reader. No reader passively accepts literary statements as his semantic sensors are ideologically charged. He reacts and responds. His tryst with the text is a meeting of two ideologies, two views and two propositions. At the meeting, agreement and disagreement are possible. However, only within the frame of the script, the dialogic process of reading can progress to the next stage of semantic synthesis. The writer, stating all he had to say in the text, lets the reader decode the signs to ferret out the meaning. The meaning is the result of a synthesis. The dialectical confrontation or consensus of the writer's and the reader's ideological positions moves on to a synthesis, eventually evolving towards a higher level of social dialogue. But it can take place only within the specific semiotic parameters, socially and arbitrarily determined. Never can a text be anarchic semiotically and be, at the same time, semantically centric. No reader can bury his author alive. Every really great author refuses to be buried alive. He is alive in his signs, in spite of his biographical absence.

Necessarily, the author-reader relationship need not be a producer-consumer relationship. Once the text has come into being, the author goes behind the curtains. His presence is latent in the ideological inscriptions in the text, the corpus of the signs. While reading, what happens is a dialogue; the absent author and the silent reader engage each other in a semantically eloquent dialogue. Reading is always dialogic. The author, hidden in the text, interpellates the reader ideologically; though impalpable, his interpellations are semantically suggestive. The dialectical (thesis-antithesis) relationship proceeds inevitably to the height of synthesis. On reading a text, the reader's consciousness, with its class ideology and character already wrought into it, confronts it [the text] as a structured set of signs. The work which offers a text to the reader is rhetorically framed and ideologically charged. Its existence is not purposeless. The intentionality of the author is a presence, made palpable through the specific selection and patterning of signs. A work is a semiotic fortress, built up sign by sign, with the author's ideological intention cementing the bricks fast and strong. Unless there are too many cracks and crevices in the base and the battlements, most of the adventurous readers will find the prison–house of language too strong for them to break out.

That the meaning of a text is always semiotically guarded is proved by a passage spoken by Rosencrantz in *the Hamlet*. In "Two Characters in *The Hamlet*: Marginalization with a Vengeance", it is stated: "Taken alone, the passage is a thoughtful and imaginatively successful passage, worthy of a wise and accomplished statesman."[10] Freed from the context, Claudius' speech on the role and power of kingship (spoken to Rosencrantz and Guildenstern, immediately after the play within the play) loses its dramatic meaning and serves another purpose. Though the passage, "intrinsically good" if looked at in isolation, is not well known because the context acts as the determinant; Rosencrantz and Guildenstern are "among the jellyfish of Shakespeare's characters". The totality of the dramatic context, marked by the various sign sequences like plot, character and dialogue determine the meaning and purpose of the passage. The semiotic structures that the playwright employs stand vigil on the reading process and compel the reader to return to dialogue.

Arthur Miller's play *The Crucible* (1952) is a retelling of the Salem witch hunt, the dramatic recreation of an aspect of American history which was marked by religious superstition, bigotry and greedy selfishness. Dramatically revisiting the events of the closing years of the 17th century Massachusetts, Miller could provide a very powerful metaphor for the political situation in America immediately after the Second World War. As the religious bigots of Salem did with those who dissented with the authority, McCarthy tried to exorcise the United States of communist witchcraft. From the timing of the production of the play, Miller's spectators could easily discern its immediate political relevance. The play has at its core the conflict between Christian religious authority and the individual's freedom to pursue any faith. What is true in the context of religion is applicable to any other political or social dogma. No spectator, whatever interpretative freedom he may grant himself, can ignore the basic conflict that is dramatically represented by different characters and their dialogue.

Every reader of Dylan Thomas's poem "Do Not Go Gentle into that Good Night" experiences the heroism of life that refuses to go into the darkness of death without a fight. It is impossible for any reader to indulge in anarchic interpretation of the text though none of its lexical terms is barred by time and place. Only towards the end of the poem, the reader understands that it is the imperative request of a son to his dying father. The night, the light, the day, the bay and the sun are all either good or gentle or sad or fierce. All are abstract and unspecific. But every reader will feel the intensity of the passion for human heroism in the face of death. The poem, a passionate plea to refuse the impending darkness of death, is an invocation to assert human dignity. Santiago in Ernest Hemingway's *The Old Man and the Sea* and Captain Ahab in Herman Melville's *Moby Dick* are certain central characters who compel the reader not to take his eyes away from them and, thereby, from the central idea of the text. That these texts have stood the test of time suggests that their semiotic organization is masterminded by the writers in such a way that they can engage the readers in perpetual dialogue.

Bakhtin does not approve of the possibility of unlimited meaning because words occur and register meaning only between two speakers. It is the social availability of signs which enable the speaker/writer and the listener/reader to use them. Both are users of linguistic signs. Deliberately, from a vast paradigm, the writer chooses the most suitable signs for effective communication and gives them a local habitation, a syntagmatic structure, a new form. The speaker has a targeted audience, an addressee. Every word/sign is a dart, aimed rhetorically at somebody, a social being. He might have sharpened the arrows and made the strings very taut before shooting. These preparations are bound to have their impact on a specific addresser. Modern novel, the most democratic of all literary genres, has its specific readers though Barthes might state that democracy has revolutionized reading. There are separate readers for detective novels and science fiction. In the days of Feudalism, when class distinctions were very sharp and evident, the elite sections of India had their Sanskrit literary forms while the lowly ones had to satisfy themselves with their folk art and literature. In Kerala, where the Namboodiri's had their Kathakali and Koodiyattam, the untouchables had their Kakkarissi and Kolkali, both genres of folk drama and folk dance respectively. The separate texts had their separate readers in mind. Bakhtin's author always recognizes the presence of a reader. He is fully convinced that every utterance is a social gesture and has a social genesis.

The language of literature comprises social words; they are not isolated or abandoned, but related and captured for specific purposes.

The reader is not an abstraction, and, reading is not a futile exercise in the social void. Social history, biography and psychology define the semiotic space of the reader. The reader's knowledge of a language, his semiotic competence, determines the text and the temper of his consciousness. Like the author, he is unconsciously shaped and shadowed by the class structure of his society. Transmitted by the author, the literary text reaches the reader whose antenna will be activated only if there is a commonly shared semiotic field. Dialogue takes place when there is a correspondence of signs. The literary signs of the Chinese offer only an unwelcome façade to the non-Chinese. The Sanskrit epics of India are impenetrable to the vast majority of Indians who are unlettered in it. Certain physical pre-conditions, like a semiotic rapport between the author and the impending reader, are essential for the enunciation of textual meaning. The linguistic signs of the text, the syntagmatic representation of an aspect of the author's consciousness, will be invulnerable to the reader who does not know the weapons of the trade. A semiotic kinship between the author and the reader is necessary to make meaning out of reading and to make reading meaningful. The 'authored text' and the 'texted reader' should be connected dialectically.

ENDNOTES

1   David Lodge, *Modern Criticism and Theory: A Reader* (London: Longman, 1990) 167-172.

2   B.Das &J. Mohanty, eds. "From Work to Text", *Literary Criticism: A Reading,*(OUP) 413-420.

3   B.Das &J. Mohanty, 416.

4   Ibid, 417.

5   Ibid, 420.

6   Roland Barthes, "The Death of the Author", *Modern Criticism and Theory -A Reader, Ed. David Lodge* (London: Longman, 1990) 171

7   Roland Barthes, "The Death of the Author", *Modern Criticism and Theory-A Reader,* 172.

8   Quoted in Katerina Clark and Michael Holquist, *Mikhail Bakhtin* (Cambridge: Harvard University Press, 1984) 214-217.

9   Katerina Clark and Michael Holquist, 214.

10   Wilfred L.Guerin, Earle Labor, et al, *A Handbook of Critical Approaches to Literature,* 4th ed. OUP, 270-275.

THE READER
AND
THE *SAHRUDAYA*

As a result of the deconstructionist shift in his semantic philosophy, Roland Barthes gave focused attention to the reader in his poststructuralist literary theory. He privileged and exalted the reader to a status higher than in earlier literary theories. His famous essay "The Death of the Author" is a celebration of the demise of the "Author-God" as it maintains; "... the text is henceforth made and read in such a way that at all its levels the author is absent"[1]. Here Barthes authorizes the Reader to be the sole custodian of meaning and interpretation of the text which is the confluence of diverse semantic codes. Thus the Barthian reader turns out to be an opponent, not the dialectical opposite, of the author (writer). The assertion of the interpretative freedom of the reader, in effect, has over-privileged him, giving him a free lease for over-interpretation. This is an unreal and anarchic situation which transforms the reader into an abstraction. In his enthusiasm to repudiate the tyranny of the author in critical practice, Barthes grants absolute hermeneutic freedom to his reader. This is quite against all common sense and critical wisdom because it ignores the fact that the text is an artefact, a logical structure of inter-locking semiotic codes.

As participants in a specific mode of mutual communication, the writer and the reader actively operate on simultaneous differences and similarities, though they have distinct qualities which distinguish them from the rest of the society. The writer and the reader, to be specific, are different from each other as well as from their social cohabitants. But, apart from the differences, there are many factors which bridge and bond the author and the reader as kindred spirits. They share identical cognitive faculties. The author and the reader are comparable as both of them are cognizant of the same linguistic (semiotic) codes. Most notably, if we adopt the functional model of Roman Jakobson, the author is at one end of the linear channel of communication as Sender and the reader is at the other end of the same channel as Receiver. And, in between them, there is the Message, framed and formulated contextually. Language, the medium, helps them share common semantic interpretative possibilities.

Language *means* only when the spoken (written) word is heard (read). Language is not for speaking (writing) only, but it is for hearing (reading) as well. All human beings, if not physiologically incapacitated in their vocal and auditory faculties, are capable of linguistic utterances and semantic comprehension. In usual social contexts, though all those who use language *do* communicate, all of them *are not* authors from the point of view of literary aesthetics. And, similarly, all those who hear language and gather information are not readers. Speak/hear, hear/speak, write/read and read/write are the dialectical binaries in linguistic communication. The ways in which the language of poetry or literary art differs from the language of ordinary speech are now well known. The use of lexical codes in literary contexts invests them with distinctive functions, often termed imaginative or emotive or poetic. Even Barthes has admitted this. He writes that the codes are so manipulated that "... a text is made of multiple writings, drawn from many cultures and entering into mutual relations of dialogue, parody, contestation..."[2] The writer, a codifier, does not use the codes of his language mechanically, but he employs them selectively and creatively. Something, quite elusive and abstract, goes into the making of the encoded message, the text. The Writer is no ordinary human being talking to other ordinary human beings. Wordsworth has said, "The Poet is a Man speaking to Men." The men to whom Wordsworth refers to here are not a heterogeneous mass, but they are his readers who can understand his language, the "language really used by men". Sensitive as they are to his language, his poems are sensible to them. They may not share his political ideas or philosophic visions or revolutionary views or romantic love of Nature, but they have the knowledge of his language that encodes all these.

The writer and the reader are not casual speakers and careless listeners. They share a common medium. The writer is no laid-back user of language; he is deliberate; he has motives; he sharpens every dart before aiming it at his target. He is no aimless archer shooting into the darkness of ignorant night. The reader, similarly, is no ordinary careless listener, an idle member of a vast hoard of people. The reader has such and so much distinction in him as to learn, understand and respond to the semiotic suggestions which target him. It should be noted that Barthes ignores the fact that the reader should be cognizant of the semiotic codes of the text to enable its reading. An enabling knowledge of the text's social, cultural and ideological composition is essential for the reader's meaningful dialogue with it. This actually brings the writer and the reader face to face. The reader can read only in the 'presence' of a writer's consciousness concretized through the semiotics of the text:

> The reader is the space on which all the quotations that makeup a writing are inscribed without any of them being lost; a text's unity lies not in its origin but in its destination. Yet this destination cannot any longer be personal: the reader is without history, biography, psychology; he is simply someone who holds together in a single field all the traces by which the written text is constituted....[3]

When Barthes accords such privileged position to the reader, whether he is doing well to the reader is a questionable fact. His abstraction of the reader, whose freedom for the interpretation of the text he claims to uphold, only helps miss the marks of his actuality. The reader is not an airy insubstantial personality. He is a concrete living being with a biography, sociology and a psychology of his own. They definitively shape the reader's consciousness, its strength and weakness to take cognizance of the semiotic events, the text. He is not naive or innocent of the ways of the world or literary art; nor is he an easy victim to the ideological overtures of the crafty author.

Besides, championing the cause of the reader, Barthes has leveled a very serious charge against all his predecessors in the field of literary criticism. "Classic criticism", Barthes writes, "has never paid any attention to reader; for it, the writer is the only person in literature."[4] Barthes charge is quite superficial and sweeping as it is not substantiated by historical facts. Though neo-classicism was limited by its inherent mechanical nature, Alexander Pope's words prove that it held the writer and the reader equivalently:

> A perfect Judge will read each work of Wit
> With the same spirit that its author writ.

Pope did not separate the Judge (the Reader or the Critic) from the Wit, the Writer. Besides, he underscored the sameness of spirit in them.

The "the sameness of spirit" of the writer and the reader, which Pope, the neo-classicist underscores distinctly reflects the concept of *the Sahrudaya* (kindred spirit), elaborately dealt with in ancient Sanskrit literary aesthetics. In fact the *Sahrudaya* concept challenges the views of the deconstructionists and, in particular, of Barthes, their ardent articulator in literary theory. Though Barthes's ideas were initially influenced by the structuralist ideas of Saussure, a scholar in the Grammar of Panini, the ancient Sanskrit grammarian, it seems, he did not have any clear idea of Sanskrit poetics and how it considered the mutuality of the author and the reader.

In India, the consideration of the reader has always been an important aspect of literary theory. Even the Vedic poets, as Kunhunni Raja notes, have stated "that only the *Sahrudayas* can enjoy the real beauty of poetry, others are like people who see, but do not find."[5]

Subsequently, not only Vedic poets, but many other literary critics have dealt with the specific qualities of the people who can identify and experience aesthetic beauty of literature. To Bhattanayaka (900-1000 AD?), from whose works Abhinavagupta and others have copiously quoted, the aesthetic relish (Rasa), can be experienced only by a person endowed with *Sahrudayasiddhi* (the qualities of a sensitive reader). Along with the discussion of the concepts of the poetic motif, the poetic form and the poet, Rajasekhara (880-920AD?) and Kuntaka (925-1020) have discussed the role of the *Sahrudaya* (Reader) respectively in *Kavyameemamsa* and V*akrokthijivitam.*

Compared to western poetics, Indian literary aesthetics has accorded a higher, a more exalted, status to the reader. As T.N. Sreekantaiya notes, "The great contribution of India to Comparative Poetics is the doctrine of *Rasa-Dhvani,* the process by which the reader re-creates for himself and re-lives the poet's original experience."[6] The *Rasa-Dhvani* (Relish-Suggestion) principle accords almost equal status to the reader and the poet: "He is the *Sahrudaya*-one with kindred heart-in whom the outpouring of the poet's heart finds its goal and fulfillment". Implicitly, Indian poetics recognizes the dialectical nature of the relationship between the poet and the reader. They are the two aspects of the *Saraswata-tattwa* (the Poetic Principle). The passage of invocation in the Dhvanyaloka Locana reads:

> *Saraswathyasthatwam kavisahrdayakhyam*
> *vijayathe.*

It means: "May the poetic principle in the poet and the reader succeed!" The *Sahrudaya* (the Reader) is equipped to receive the imaginative outpouring from the heart of the poet. The Creative Imagination (the *Karayitri Pratibha*), according to Rajasekhara meets the Responsive Imagination (the *Bhavayitri Pratibha*) of the reader. Unless the poet and the reader are on the same wave length of semiotic codes, the poetic experience, rendered in terms of imaginative language will not simply take place. There should be similarity-*samaanatha*-between the poet's creative faculty and the reader's appreciative potential. Within the all-important *Rasa t*heory, the space that the poet and the reader occupy is not mutually exclusive.

In this respect, Indian poetics is in vast disagreement with the 'reader-centeredness' of Barthes which is, in comparison, a mechanical search for not-so-apparent shades of meaning of the textual signs. Barthes misses the vital principle of Imagination, the poet's mental faculty that enlivens the chosen language. He also misses the point that the reader imaginatively responds to the semiotic suggestions in the literary work. Reading is not a cold process of detecting the traces of visible and invisible signs as per Derrida's semantic logic; but it is a warm, organic, imaginative endeavor of creation and re-creation where kindred spirits-the author and the reader- dialectically engage each other. In this the reader not only recaptures and relives the poet's experience, but also, with a sense of dialectical fraternity, goes beyond the apparent in search of new semantic realms.

The Rasa-Dhvani theory of Indian poetics refutes Barthes charge that classic literary criticism did not accord deserving importance to the reader. But whatever it is with the literary or critical heritages of other nationalities, indisputably, the reader has unique importance in Indian poetics. The genesis of the reader takes place only when the work reaches him. As the reader is also cognizant of the semiotic codes in which the experiences of life are meditated upon and made manifest in the literary text, his creative imagination can, sometimes, soar up to heights never imagined by even the poet. As Mohan Thampi says, the *Sahrudaya* is a Leavisite 'complete reader', critic and aesthetician, rolled into one:

> A competent reader is expected to have (i) a large fund of experience, and (ii) a trained sensibility. He must be an able observer capable of making appropriate deductions from the interactions of images and characters in the poem.... [7]

The importance given to the reader (*Sahrudaya*) in Indian Poetics is not lopsided as the creation and the enjoyment of *Rasa* (Supreme Poetic Pleasure) is the concern of both the author and the reader. The similarity of the imaginative principle pervading them positions them in the same channel of communication as the Sender and the Receiver of the linguistic codes.

It is Mikhail Bakhtin's dialogic principle that comes closest to the Indian literary principle that binds the poet and the reader in union: *Saraswatyatvam kavisahrudayakhyam*. Bakhtin's dialogic principle resolves the problem of lopsided reader-centeredness in Western Literary Theory. He makes the author-reader relationship mutual and dialectical. The author and the reader are caught in semiotic mutuality. It is not the author or the reader who makes meanings; meaning arises from the dialectical union of the reader's and the author's consciousness on the plains of the literary work.

Bakhtin's major works deal with the dialogic quality of language and the semiotic quality of discourse. He has evolved a new science of language which he calls Translinguistics and the Poetics of Utterance.[8] He was always opposed to the idea of the singularity of truth in the world as he had a mind that relished the plenitude and plurality of differences. He emphasized the cognitive and the social in language and discerned the structures of interpersonal relations in a "world in between consciousness" and invested such terms as 'dialogue' and 'utterance' with a new meaning. Dialogue is not a conversation between two people, but "a communication" under "extensive set of conditions" "between simultaneous differences". Like Barthes, who found liberty in the interrogative possibility of the literary language, Bakhtin grounded it "in the dialogic nature of language and society."

According to Bakhtin, meaning is the product of dialectical interactions. The word is a territory shared by the speaker (addresser) and the listener (addressee)[9] The word exists only in a dialogic context that is always part of history. Discourse is always inter-individual:

> Language acquires life and historically evolves precisely here, in concrete verbal communication, and not in the abstract linguistic system of language forms, nor in the individual psyche of speakers[10]

Only between two speakers differences in meaning can be registered. Always a word is targeted towards an addressee. Whereas grammar tends to systematize a language, contexts of language resist order and organization. Bakhtin writes:

> ...the word is a two-sided act. It is determined equally by whose word it is and for whom it is meant. A word, it is precisely the product of the reciprocal relationship between speaker and listener, addresser and addressee....A word is a bridge thrown between myself and another... it is a territory shared by both addresser and addressee[11].

Bakhtin considered language as the stage where different social accents are voiced. It is the interaction of the social forces that brings a word into being. Language is the product of the social milieu. A speech is a discourse in action. All speech is rhetorical and, therefore, ideological and semiotic. Only in inter-individual territory a sign can *be and mean.* A word and an experience are made what they are by the meaning they communicate. It is "theme" which makes them distinct and theme is characterized by varying contexts. Bakhtin understands the dialectical relationship between theme and meaning, the two building blocks of utterance. A person who considers an utterance has to deal with the otherness of the whole situation. According to him any true understanding is dialogic in nature and meaning is realized only in the process of active, responsive understanding. Meaning is, as Katerina Clarke and Michael Holquist state, "not in the word or in the soul of the speaker or in the soul of the listener. Meaning is the effect of interaction between speaker and listener produced via the material of a particular sound complex"[12].

Bakhtin's Dialogism convincingly rebuts the anarchy of interpretation unleashed by the post-structuralists led by Derrida and fought out by Barthes. A literary text is the semiotic manifestation of an aspect of its author's consciousness. A reader or an interpreter who confronts it is likely to bring in his ideas while dealing with it. Naturally, there ensues a dialogue between the text, the structured consciousness of the author, and the interpreter. The thesis meets its antithesis and a resultant synthesis evolves which is the meaning. Neither the total negation of the authorial consciousness, nor the total domination of the interpreter's consciousness takes place. Dialogue moves on to another level and it moves on to new boundaries.

The ideas of Bakhtin and the *Sahrudaya* concept of Sanskrit are implicitly ratified by Wolfgang Iser, the proponent of the Reader Response Theory who distinguishes between the 'work' and the 'text'.[13] When the text and the reader converge, "the literary work" comes into existence:

> As the reader uses the various perspectives offered him by the text in order to relate the patterns and the 'schematized views to one another, he sets the work in motion, and this very process results ultimately in the awakening of responses within himself.... If reading removes the subject-object division that constitutes all perception, it follows that the reader will be 'occupied' by the thoughts of the author, and these in turn will cause the drawing of new 'boundaries'....Here in lies the dialectical structure of reading.

Terry Eagleton has endorsed the view of Bakhtin and Iser which are in consonance with the *Sahrudaya* concept of Sanskrit poetics. The reader who approaches a text with pre-formed ideas is subjected to interrogation and it, in return, is interrogated by the literary text. Both are mutually unsettled, 'disconfirmed' and transformed. This is possible only if the reader has "some grasp of its 'codes', by which is meant the rules which systematically govern the ways it produces its meanings."[14]

ENDNOTES

1   Roland Barthes, "The Death of the Author", *Issues in Contemporary Critical Theory*, ed. Peter Barry (London: Macmillan, 1987) 53-55.

2   David Lodge, *Modern Criticism and Theory; A Reader*, (London: Longman, 1990) 171.

3   Ibid, 171.

4   Ibid, 171.

5   Kuhunni Raja, "The Literary Value of the Rgveda" (trans.) *The literary History of Sanskrit,* eds. K.Kuhunni Raja and M.S.Menon (Trichur: Kerala Sahitya Academy, 1990) 77.

6   T.N.Sreekantaiiya, "Imagination in Indian Poetics", *Indian Aesthetics*, ed. V.S.Sethuraman (Macmillan: Madras, 1992) 219-234.

7   Mohan Thampi, "Rasa as Aesthetic Experience:The Rasa-sutra", *Indian Aesthetics*, ed. V.S.Sethuraman, (Madras: Macmillan, 1992) 320.

8   Mikhail Bakhtin, *The Bakhtin Reader: Selected Writings of Bakhtin,* Medvedev and Volosinov, ed. Pam Morris (London: Edward Arnold, 1994) 35.

9   Mikhail Bakhtin, *Marxism and Philosophy of Language,* trans. Ladislav Matejka and I.R.Titunik (New York: Seminar Press, 1973) 85-86

10   *Bakhtin Reader,* 59.

11   Mikhail Bakhtin, *Marxism and Philosophy of Language,* 85-86.

12   Katerina Clark and Michael Holquist, *Mikhail Bakhtin* (Cambridge: Harvard Univ. Press, 1984) 232.

13   Wolfgang Iser, "Reception Theory", *Issues in Contemporary Critical Theory,* ed. Peter Barry (London: Macmillan, 1987) 119-127.

14   Terry Eagleton, "Reception Theory", *Issues in Contemporary Critical Theory,* ed. Peter Barry (London: Macmillan, 1987) 123.

THE POLITICAL PHILOSOPHY OF TRANSLATION

Translation, apparently a linguistic process that seeks semantic equivalence for ideological articulations in another language, has latent political and cultural implications. The modern geopolitics of globalization has made it a more complex activity than it has ever been in the past. The insidious economic design of globalization insistently repeats that the absence of an international language is the biggest obstacle to the furtherance of free trade and commerce world-wide. Its totalizing invasiveness does not leave regional languages alone, but systematically imposes Anglo-American English on them as the most suitable global medium for the transaction of goods and services. This cry for a common universal language is, in fact, an attempt to cover up the exploitative nature of globalization. It is pointed out that the rapid development in transport and digital communication has shrunk the world into an inclusive village where linguistic uniformity is inevitable for progress. The campaign for Anglo-American English has created a general impression that the diversity of languages is an avoidable nuisance. In effect, a battle of languages is waged in the global theatre of political economy. But it is often forgotten that no language can defeat another linguistically and that the battle of languages is not fought in linguistics, but in politics. The death of a language is the result of the political death of the people speaking it.

However, when, in this way, Anglo-American English, the language of hegemonic global power, compels linguistic and cultural homogenization, other languages instinctively combat it and struggle for survival. And translation, thus, becomes a sword and a shield, a political weapon for defensive resistance. More than a neutral transfer of meaning, translation becomes a motivated linguistic and cultural exercise in which class interests run into each other for ideological dominance.

In a conflict-ridden society, language becomes dense with cultural signs and ideological designs. And, as a result, the common social status of language, as in the case of wealth, becomes indistinguishable[1]. A historical study of translation is sufficient to validate the political intention of translations and translators. The earliest translations were royal edicts and whether they were of Emperor Sargon (3000 B.C.) or of Hammurabi (2600 B.C.) or of Asoka (304-232 B.C), they were assertions of imperial resolve and authority. Very subtle social and political intentions could be discerned in the numerous translations of Greco-Roman books into European languages during the Renaissance.

The cultural politics of translation gets highly pronounced when we historically move over to the translations of the Bible. When the 'Old Testament' of Hebrew Jews was translated for Greek-speaking

Jews, the obvious political plan was racial unification, rather than religious. But, later, when the entire Judea fell under Roman domination, there appeared several translations of the Bible in Latin, the language of the victorious Romans. As Christianity became the religion of the Roman Empire, naturally, Latin became the official language, of politics and of religion. In due course, Feudal Roman Catholic Church insisted on the untranslatability of Latin Bible in order to preserve its economic and political dominance. As Latin was the language of the state and religion, any linguistic allowance would ultimately lead to the dissolution of the state power, it was feared.

However, in subsequent years, the dissolution of medieval Feudalism dialectically paved the way for numerous translations of the Bible. John Wycliff (1330-1384), "the Morning Star of Reformation", translated it into English for teaching Christian values to ordinary people. Martin Luther's (1483-1546) German translation gave an impetus to the development of capitalism and hastened the spread of Protestantism. When William Tyndale (1494-1536) translated the 'New Testament' into English, his aim was different from that of the Catholic priests, who treated the Holy Book as their prerogative. At this juncture, the translator was not merely a scholar in languages and religion; he was a political activist, endowed with economic views and social visions.

As the Catholic Church feared the translation of the Bible would erode its authority, it tried to dissuade the translators by persecuting them mercilessly. Wycliff and Tyndale were burned alive not just for casting seeds of revolt against Feudalism, but for breeding religious dissent in addition. But, however the Church authorities tried, the laity could not be prevented from seeking the word of God in their own tongue. As more and more translations of the Bible appeared, there arose a situation when an individual could communicate directly with his God in his own language and without the mediation of the Catholic priest and his Latin. Thus translation of the Bible into different provincial languages hastened the spirit of Protestantism and the pace of democracy[2]. When capitalism assumed colonial proportions and patronized Christian values, European Missionaries got an opportunity to translate the Bible into the languages of the colonies. For this they had to study regional languages and compile dictionaries in them. The colonial powers used translation not only for exercising administrative and political authority, but also for ideological manipulations, religious and political.

The inter-lingual relationship in ancient, colonial and post-colonial India should be understood against the tradition of class conflict epitomized in the dictum: *Soodramakshara samyuktham doorayeth parivarjayeth,* which means the literate low-caste should be discarded far away. The *Avarnas* (those who did not belong to the four *Varnas*) were proscribed from paths along which even wild cats and dogs could stride or stroll freely. Also they were excluded from the world of letters and knowledge. In *na sthree soodram vedam adheeyatham* the denial of knowledge to women and *soodras* is clearly pronounced. The totalizing authority of Brahmanism did not allow any osmotic relationship between Sanskrit and other languages. Only when the Feudal production relations were shaken during the Middle Ages (1200—1500), Sanskrit began to communicate with other Indian languages. The observation of K. Damodaran that "the regional languages received encouragement when Sanskrit literature suffered decline" is very significant[3]. The impacts of Buddhism, Jainism, Islam and the Bhakti Movement had effectively weakened the stranglehold of Brahmnical Sanskrit, the language of knowledge and power, on other languages. Under the influence of the Bhakti movement, religious classics like *the Ramayana, the Maha Bharata, the Bhagavat Gita* and other Sanskrit books, were translated into the regional languages like Hindi, Tamil, Kannada and Malayalam. The political and social essence of India, celebrated as "unity in diversity", began to in-form the Indian sensibility through translations from Sanskrit. The universal values enshrined in Sanskrit comprise the treasures that enrich and energize the political unity of India.

The British Raj exercised its colonial dominance in India for more than a century and a half and offered favorable conditions for the use of English in administration and education. Unlike the Brahmins who had denied the use and knowledge of Sanskrit language to the vast exploited masses, the colonial British deliberately nurtured a race of disciples and descendants from among Indians, teaching them English language and western values. In either case the purpose was class exploitation and segregation. The Christian missionaries, with the patronage of the colonial administration, taught English language as part of their efforts at the religious conversion of the Hindus. They studied Indian vernaculars diligently and engaged themselves in translations. These translations, undoubtedly, from Sanskrit to English and from English to Indian languages resulted in the rediscovery of Sanskrit and the modernization of Indian languages. But an unexpected fall-out of English education was the dissemination of scientific temper and the creation of democratic consciousness in India.

When English was introduced to multilingual India, there were contradictory reactions. With the triumphant pride of a victor, in his Minutes of 1835, Lord Macaulay condemned the literature of Sanskrit as worthless and recommended the study of English. But on the other hand William Jones valued the treasures of Sanskrit with a sense of awful wonder and admiration. In fact, the literary pursuit of translation had its most fruitful harvest and gleaning in India during the struggle for independence. The observation of K. Damodaran on this is very relevant:

> Many European and Indian scholars turned their eyes back on their own past and translated Sanskrit texts on different subjects and wrote original works to wake up the spirit of Nationalism. Their main aim was to establish that Indian culture was not second to any other culture. Thus there arose, quite contrary to what the British imperialists had expected, a new sense of patriotism and national progress in the Indian mind. These new stirrings influenced not only the literatures of Indian languages and philosophy, but also impacted on Indian political thought. India stepped into modern age[4].

The perspectives of the Indians and the British on translation were contradictory. Through translation the British tried to amass the knowledge of Sanskrit and other Indian languages. Besides, they used it for obvious political dominance. Appropriation of India's wealth and subjugation of the Indians were the aims of the British linguistic policy and translation practice. But to the Indian students of English, the acquisition of western science, technology, philosophy, political theory, etc. and their dissemination was the chief, if not the only, end of translation. To them translation was an instrument of struggle against colonialism. The imperialists had never expected that the study of English language, which they had introduced for administrative convenience, would ultimately dig their own political grave, cultivating anti-colonial feelings in the Indian mind[5].

Usually, in class-divided societies, the subjugated are reduced to subservient positions and are ideologically conditioned to copy the walk and talk of their governors. They put on the mental chain of loyalty that rings in their languages as eloquent political markers. On the conquest of England by William of Orange in 1066 A.D., the British courtiers had readily started studying Norman French in order to voice their allegiance to the French crown. In colonial India, dialectically, on the one hand, English language had inspired cultural resistance and nationalist struggle, and, on the other, it had engendered an elite aloofness among those who were loyal to their colonial overlords. The British could domesticate a section of the educated and make them their faithful vassals. The observation of Dr. J. P. Naik that the British education had performed three kinds of political functions in India is factually true: *domination, domestication, and liberation*[6]. More than any other political leader of the Nationalist period, Mahatma Gandhi was acutely conscious of the class division that English language was creating in Indian society. Gandhi noted that educated Indians had a great affinity to English more than to their mother tongue.[7] This deep social chasm was the consequence of increased class conflict.

The class division that Mahatma Gandhi painfully observed persists in 'post-independent' or 'post colonial' India as an ever widening economic disparity. So far there has never been any radical reconsideration of the relationship between English and the Indian languages. Truly the regional languages of India have developed greatly after the reunification of the states on the basis of language. Within the Indian Union the states now co-exist and co-operate in a healthy manner without any vested hegemonic political motive corrupting their relationship. Besides, beyond the binary premises of donor / recipient, the languages function fraternally as the national political atmosphere is quite conducive to it. But, when Santha Ramakrishna considers the relationship among present day Indian languages to substantiate her thesis of linguistic hegemony in class society, it should be submitted that the example is inexact as it betrays lack of proper class consciousness[8]. In India all languages recognized under the Constitution coexist and function on equal terms. No linguistic state has any right or opportunity to exercise any kind of political or economic or linguistic authority over any other state. Therefore, the reference to Indian states as proof of the argument that the dominant class, which wields economic and political authority, has linguistic and cultural upper-hand is totally incorrect. The relationship prevailing among Indian languages is not an example good enough to substantiate the hegemonic theory of languages. Without political hegemony no linguistic hegemony is possible and, in India, no state has political hegemony over any other state.

Unfortunately, independent India is not post, but pro colonial, compelling us to recall Gandhiji's anxious observation. Even after attaining political sovereignty India has not outlived her colonial heritage. In the absence of radical cultural de-colonization, English continues to be the language for class dominance in India, as the ruling elite sections have accorded pre-eminence to English in education and administration. How the positions of the author and the subject are determined in linguistic relationship is based on the nature of mutuality between the people who speak those languages. It was not because of any linguistic virtuosity that colonial English could gain a more dominant position in India than Sanskrit or Urdu; the English people had political dominance and, therefore, their language could be the voice of power and authority. The attitude of the English to the Indians during the colonial days was the same as that of the French, the Spanish and the Portuguese to their colonial subjects. The experiences of Goa and Pondicherry prove this. In the political situation available then, the reciprocal mind-sets of the authoritative benefactor and the devoted beneficiary were unavoidable. Therefore, often, the translation from the regional languages into English, the language of the colonial master, was a humble demonstration of loyalty and a polite offering for approval and recognition.

When the imperialism of the 19th and 20th centuries revisits us now in the form of globalization, the inherent class conflict is more intense and complex than it had ever been in the past. To ensure its dominance over science, technology, economy, media, etc. for ever, Anglo-American English, the lingua franca of globalization, seeks control over all aspects of language and translation. George Steiner who tried to compose 'a poetics of translation' has specially discussed how the authoritarian ascendancy of English over other languages is pushing the languages of Africa and Amazonia into premature death and extinction[9]. Steiner is afraid that, when under the spell of market economy English brushes aside other languages, it will lose its own ability to address reality creatively. The new English of global commerce will destroy not only the natural vitality and cultural autonomy of native languages, but it will also degenerate to the level of the Esperanto, the artificial international language devised by L.L. Zamenhof (1859-1977), a Polish physician. The artificial languages with limited number of words and syntactic structures may be enough for net surfing and s.m.s., but it is quite inadequate for the semantic contexts of life lived away from digital virtuality. As Steiner laments, globalization has made the English of Shakespeare and Shelly mere Pidgin. The celebration of the festival of world languages is spoilt by the semantic grunginess of Anglo-American English.

Steiner has also suggested that we should realize the political philosophy of language and translation. Though physiologically all human beings are similar, through thousands of languages they assume differences. The attempt to brand the plurality of language as undesirable 'anarchy' is motivated by the undemocratic and dictatorial villainy of corporate fascism. It is language which enables man to survive inimical natural phenomena and inevitable death, the greatest of biological limitations. The ability to address reality imaginatively is possible only through language[10]. Beyond the bounds of individual mortality, language is the only vital nectar, the philosophical life blood of human survival. Each language has a separate world of its own. Each language inscribes the world in its own way. When a language dies, a world dies along with it[11]. Therefore, not to die, the world should live its languages.

But globalization has hastened the death of many languages. With the help of global market and technocracy, Anglo-American English exercises deterrent sovereignty on other languages. The failure of the socialist nations to survive the incursions of neo-capitalism has resulted in the linguistic hegemony of American English. The winding up of the Russian language teaching centers in India is a reminder of the relationship between language and politics. Nowadays, all undeveloped and developing nations use English as an escalator to the heights of socio-economic development.

Language is an inscription of human consciousness. Therefore, every effort at translation is an attempt to take in that specific aspect of human consciousness inscribed in a language, finding semantic equivalence for it in another language. Language is, simultaneously, consciousness and its concrete manifestation. Man's dialectical relationship with reality is made creative in and by language. Generating alternities of being, language helps man refute the imperatives of Nature; it helps him reflect on his selfhood and identity. Each individual has a language-an idiolect. In this sense what happens in language is individuation. Each language provides an interpretation of life. Therefore, when we move from one language to another through translation, we are moving from one life to another, from one world to another. Translation is the great effort of an individual to move from the privacy of the self; it breaks the limitations of language; it leads the individual from the limited experiences of his world. Translation is an individual's great endeavor to take cognizance of the life of others; it is his emotional internalization of their being. The politics of this struggle for freedom is the soul of translation in its atomic and massive senses.

A philosophic translator always realizes the political content and practical intent of translation. The books received for translation may be the result of diverse ideological interests. Books can be written for mere information transfer or for propagation of ideas or for creative reflections on experiences. Books with specific rhetorical purpose may try to influence others through their subtle politics. Hitler's *Mein Kampf,* Anne Frank's 'Diary' and the autobiographies of Mahatma Gandhi and Golwalker are good examples of the ideological diversities in literary works. Of these which book is worth selection is an existential issue that is totally dependent on the disposition and the sense of freedom of the concerned individual. And, logically, which literary work the individual translator chooses is an indication of his political vision.

At this juncture, the translator's philosophical position, rhetorical potential and political partisanship become problematic. The translator can be a translating machine. As in machine translations, quite mechanically, he can transfer ideas from one language to another and be at peace with himself. A person who carries out translation keeping pace with the speed of printing machines is no philosophical translator at all. A mechanical translator cannot impart the dimension of political creativity to his translation.

The philosopher-translator understands socio-political processes historically and keeps progressive social transformation always in view. About the social structure he has clear visions; his translation projects are envisioned by concepts which would ensure social equity and justice. He is no neutral or indifferent carrier or courier. He is very much interested in the process of social transformation. Seeking qualitative social change, he discovers adequate resources in the source language and considers it his obligation to recreate them honestly in the target language. There are elements of inquiry, discovery and recreation in the translation process. Translation becomes a creative social praxis by virtue of its politics.

The man of letters cannot stage a political revolution all by himself. But literature can creatively energize revolutionary processes with the great principles of which it is the vehicle. In providing Kerala a distinct socio-political status, the social reformers, the Renaissance leaders, the nationalist and the leftist politicians had played a great role. But the role of literary works, especially translations, in the social revolution is no small thing. From the days when

Kessari Balakrishna Pillai showed the way to foreign literature, the works of English, French and Russian authors were the sources of inspiration to the educated among the people of Kerala. The literary works of writers like Guy de Maupassant, Emile Zola, Honore' Balzac, Charles Dickens, Leo Tolstoy, Thomas Hardy, Maxim Gorky, Mikhail Sholokhov, Fydor Dostoevsky, Alexander Pushkin and Ivan Turgenev, the political and philosophical texts of Karl Marx, Friedrich Engels and Vladimir Lenin were tremendous influences on the people of Kerala. The works well received in Kerala were socially and politically important ones. Great writers like Premchand and Yashpal from Hindi, Bankim Chnadra Chatterjee, Rabindra Nath Tagore, Tara Shankar Banerjee, Bimal Mitra and Savitry Roy from Bengali, Sivarama Karanth and Niranjana from Kannada, K.M.Munshi from Marathi became much adored literary figures to Keralites because of the social and political content of their works.

When translation acquires a political perspective, it adds new connotations to the social notion of 'culture'. As each people have a language and, therefore, a culture, it is strongly argued that just as language, cultural identity should also be preserved and protected. Like language, culture is also a process. Acting diachronically and synchronically on socio-economic stages in human life, each evolutionary process leads us up to a progressive future. Cultural processes are also liable to evolution. But many people view certain rituals, life styles and forms of expressions that are relatively stagnant as unchanging cultural identities. They glorify them indiscriminately. They obstinately insist that they should be maintained eternally without any change affecting them. In their consideration of culture, politics is not a subject at all. Therefore, socio-economic structures do not form a part of their thoughts on culture. The strenuous efforts in different parts of the world for bringing about socialism and social justice do not form a part of any cultural process according to them. But even Barbara Godard, who discusses the relationship between translation and literature, does not see politics as a part of class struggle, but only as part of power relations[12]. Freedom, Democracy, Fraternity, Equality, Social Justice, etc. are the dynamic driving forces behind social perspectives and social processes. How these get marked in each language is part of a translator's enquiry. The search to identify those forces of class hegemony that stand in the way of making these great values socially possible is also part of this enquiry. The struggle against the language-politics of globalization is now treated as the 'agitativeness' of language. The communication of this through translation is the progressive political mission of a philosophic translator.

Viewed against this perspective, the argument that the purpose of translation is the creation of cultural harmony among people speaking different languages is too simple a view of the whole issue. In a country like India where diverse linguistic and cultural nationalities interact, to argue that translations will help reduce social tensions and linguistic conflicts is to deduce a moral by that tale and to reduce the translator to a traffic cop on the high way of culture[13].

Really, when we discuss the political perspective of translation, certain basic changes are required in our linguistic attitudes. In the modern context of totalizing globalization - the class politics of the violation of national languages by Anglo-American English - translation cannot but be part of class politics. As the impact of globalization deepens, the resistance against it also gains force and intensity. It is necessary for translation to identify the struggle against the neo-colonial forces in different places and in different languages, and to build up a united front against the forces of colonialism.

In this regard, the proposal of Gayatri Chakravorty Spivak is salutary and worth following[14]. Spivak views translation as part of the Feminist agenda that cherishes the solidarity of women all over the world. Translation helps understand the feminists' works in those languages. She suggests the study and translation of the language of the oppressed people of the third world nations. Through translation, which is intimate and offers intense reading, the experiences of the women of those languages can be communicated with others. Instead of translating from English or other European languages which are the linguistic organs of globalization, the class solidarity established through translation with those who suffer linguistic and cultural subalternity will surely strengthen the struggle against it.

The biblical story of the Tower of Babel is a mythical elucidation of the politics of language and translation. To frustrate the aims of the humans, who had tried to reach heaven by building a tower at Babel, God had cast disunity among them through different languages[15]. The God of the myth is a metaphor for political authority, a power center that disseminates disunity through diversity of languages. Therefore, translation is a revolt, a linguistic refutation of divine authority that disunites the humans. Each translation is a political action, an epistemic attempt to exalt ourselves from the disunity of ignorance to the unity of knowledge. Translation is not the mechanical process of detecting semantic equivalents for the linguistic codes of the source language in another language. Breaking up the opacity of linguistic signs, translation aims at the creation of a cultural awareness which is political in depth and dimension. Beyond the identification of the mutuality of languages and the transfer of ideas therein, the realistic recognition of the human situation and the struggle for the communistic alternative of human equality and unity are also part of the new translation perspective.

END NOTES

1   J.V.Stalin, *Marxism and Problems of Linguistics* (Peking: Foreign Language Press, 1976) 10.

2   Susan Bassnett, "History of Translation Theory", *Translation Studies,* 1980. Rev.Edn. (London: Routledge, 1991) 39-75.

3   K. Damodaran, *Bharatheeya Chintha (Indian Thought),* (Thiruvanathapuram: State Institute of Languages, 1973) 250.

4   K.Damodaran, *Bharatheeya Chintha (Indian Thought),* 413.

5   Santha Ramakrishnan, *Translation and Multilingualism: Post Colonial Contexts* ((Delhi: Perfect International, 1997) 17.

6   Dr. J.P.Naik, "The Political Content of Education", *The Political content of Education,* Papers submitted to the seminar organized by Academy of Political and social Studies (Pane, 1977) 1-16.

7   Santha Ramakrishnan, *Translation and Multilingualism: Post colonial Contexts.*

8   Santha Ramakrishnan, *Translation and Multilingualism: Post colonial contexts.*

9   George Steiner, *After Babel: Aspects of Language and Translation,* 3rd ed. (OUP, 1998) iv

10 George Steiner, *After Babel: Aspects of Language and Translation,* xvii.

11 George Steiner, *After Babel: Aspects of Language and Translation,* iv

12 Barbara Godard, "Culture as Translation", *Translation and Multilingualism: Post Colonial Contexts* ((Delhi: Perfect International, 1997)

13 Indranath Choudri, Plurality of Language and Literature", *Translation and Multilingualism*, 31

14 Gayatri Chakravorty Spivak, "Politics of Translation", Wikipedia, the free encyclopedia.

15 *Genesis* II: 19

SELECT BIBLIOGRAPHY

Althusser, Louis. *Lenin and Philosophy and Other Essays*. New York: Monthly Review Press, 1971.

Allott, Miriam. *Selections from Matthew Arnold*. London: J M Dent & Sons, 1 978

Arnold, Matthew. *Essays in Criticism* 2nd series. London: St.Martin's Press, 1966

Barthes, Roland. *The Semiotic Challenge*. Oxford: Basil Blackwell, 1988.

Barry, Peter. *Issues in Contemporary Critical Theory: A Casebook*. London: Macmillan, 1987.

Bassnett, Susan. *Translation Studies*. 1980. Rev.Edn. London: Routledge, 1991.

Belsey, Catherine. *Critical Practice*. London: Methuen, 1980.

Bennett, Tony. *Formalism and Marxism*. London: Methuen, 1981.

Bond, Edward. "Bingo: Scenes o Money and Death", *Plays 3*. London: Methuen, 1987.

Borev, Yuri. *Aesthetics: A Text Book*. Moscow: Progress Publishers, 1981.

Burns, Elizabeth and Tom Burns, *Sociology of Literature and Drama: Selected Readings*. Harmondsworth: Penguin Books, 1973.

Caudwell, Christopher. *Illusion and Reality: A Study of the Sources of Poetry*. 1937. Rpt. New Delhi: People's Publishing House, 1981.

Clark, Katerina and Michael Holquist. *Mikhail Bakhtin*. Cambridge: Harward U P, 1984.

Collini, Stefan, ed. *Interpretation and Overinterpretation*. Cambridge: Cambridge U P, 1992.

Craig, David. *Marxists on Literature: An Anthology*. Harmondsworth: Penguin Books, 1975.

Culler, Jonathan. *Structuralist Poetics: Structuralism, Linguistics and the Study of Literature*. New York. Cornell U P, 1975.

Culler, Jonathan. *Framing of the Sign*. Oxford: Basil Blackwell, 1986.

Damodaran, K. *Bhararatheeya Chintha (Indian Thought)*. Thiruvananthapuram: State Institute of Languages, 1973.

Das, B & J.Mohanty. *Literary Criticism: A Reading*. Calcutta: OUP1985.

De, Sushil Kumar. *Some Problems of Sanskrit Poetics.* Calcutta: FIRMA KLM Private Ltd., 1981

Derrida, Jacques. *Of Grammatology.* Delhi: Motilal Banarasidas Publishers, 1994.

Dictionary of Philosophy. 2nd rev. ed. Moscow: Progress Publishers, 1984.

Eagleton, Terry. *Literary Theory: An Introduction.* 1983. Rpt. London: Basil Blackwell, 1985.

.... *Ideology: An Introduction.* London: Verso, 1991.

.... *Marxism and Literary Criticism.* London: Methuen, 1976.

Engels, Friedrich. *Dialectics of Nature.* Moscow: Progress Publishers, 1954.

Fundamentals of Marxist-Leninist Philosophy. Moscow: Progress Publishers, 1985.

Gorky, Maxim. *On Literature.* Moscow: Progress Publishers, n.d.

Gramsci, Antonio. *Selections from the Prison Notebooks of Antonio Gramsci.* Ed. and trans. Quintin Hoare and Geoffrey Nowell Smith. New York: International Publishers, 1971.

Guerin, Wilfred L. & Earle Labor, et al. *A Handbook of Critical Approaches to Literature.*, 4th ed. OUP

Guryev. Dmtri. *The Riddle of the Origin of the Consciousness.* Moscow: Progress Publisers, 1990.

Harrison, G.B. A Book of English Poetry. Rpt. Harmondsworth: Penguin Books, 1965.

Hawkes, Terence. *Structuralism and Semiotics.* 1977. Rpt. London: Methuen, 1986.

Hill, Christopher. *Milton and the English Revolution.* London: Faber and Faber, 1977.

Ilitskaya, Lenina, tr. *ABC of Dialectical and Historical Materialism.* Moscow: Progress Publishers, 1978

Huberman, Leo. *Man's Worldly Goods.* 1946. Rpt. New Delhi: People's Publishing House, 1981.

Jakobson, Roman. *Six Lectures on Sound and Meaning.* Massachusetts: The MIT Press, 1978.

James, Scott. *The Making of Literature.* London: Mercury Books, 1963.

Jump, J.D. *From Dickens to Hardy.* 1958; rpt. London: Penguin Books, 1970.

Kermode, Frank. *The Tempest.* 1954. Rpt. London: Routledge, 1988.

Kirilenko, Galina and Lydia Korshunova. *What is Philosophy?* Moscow: Progress Publishers, 1985.

Krishnamoorthy, K. *Essays in Sanskrit Criticism.* 1964. 2nd ed. Dharwar: Karnataka University, 1974.

Leith, Dick and George Meyerson. *The Power of Address: Explorations in Rhetoric*. London: Routledge, 1989.

Lenin, V.I. *On Socialist Ideology and Culture*. 1962. Rpt. Moscow: Progress Publishers, 1978.

.... *On Literature and Art*, 1967. Rpt. Moscow: Progress Publishers, 1978.

.... *Marx, Engels, Marxism*. 1934. Rpt. Moscow: Progress Publishers, 1973.

Lodge, David. *Modern Criticism and Theory: A Reader*. London: Longman, 1990.

Lukas, Georg. History and Class Consciousness. 94. Rpt. London: Merlin Press,1983.

Lyons, John. *Language and Linguistics*: *An In Introduction*. Cambridge: Univ. Press, 1981.

Marx, Karl and Friedrich Engels. *Manifesto of the Communist Party* Moscow: Progress Publishers, 1975,

Marx, Karl and Frederick Engels. *The German Ideology*. Moscow: Progress Publishers, 1976.

Marx, Karl and Friedrich Engels. *Articles on Britain*. Moscow: Progress Publishers, 1975.

Mohan, G.B. "Marxian Literary Theory", *Social Scientist*. 8 Dec. 1979-Jan 1980: 8-29.

Morris, Pam. *The Bakhtin Reader: Selected Writings of Bakhtin, Medvedev and Volosinov.* London: Edward Arnold, 1974.

Norris, Christopher. *Deconstruction: Theory and Practice.* London: Methuen, 1982.

Novice, Sassily. *Artistic Truth and Dialectics of Creative Work.* Moscow: Progress Publishers, 1981.

Page, Adrian, ed. *The Death of the Playwright.* London: Macmillan, 1992.

Podostnik, V. and O.Yakhot. *A Brief Course of Dialectical Materialism.* Moscow: Progress Publishers, n.d.

Political Content of Education. Calcutta:, Socioresearch Publications Center, 1977.

Rajagopalan, R. *Environment: An Illustrated Quarterly.* New Delhi: OUP, 2011.

Raja, Kunhunni & M.S.Menon, eds. *The Literary History of Sanskrit.* Trichur: Kerala Sahitya Akademy,

Ramaswami, S and Seturaman, V.S. *The Critical Tradition.* Madras: Macmillan, 1978.

Ramakrishnan, Santha. *Translation and Multilingualism: Post Colonial Contexts.* Delhi: Perfect International, 1997.

Richards, I.A. *The Philosophy of Rhetoric.* London: OUP, 1936.

Ricouer, Paul. *The Rule of Metaphor.* London: Routledge and Kegan Paul, 1977.

Roy, Arundhati. *Power Politics: The Reincarnation of Rumpelstiltskin.* Kottayam: D C Books, 2001.

Sartre, Jean-Paul. *Existentailism and Human Emotions.* New York: Castle, n.d.

Seturaman, V.S. ed. *Indian Aesthetics.* Madras: Macmillan, 1992.

Simon, Roger. *Gramsci's Political Thought: An Introduction.* 1982; Rpt. London: Lawrence Wishart, 1988.

Slaughter, Cliff. *Marxism, Ideology and Literature.* London: Macmillan, 1980.

Stalin, J.V. *Marxism and Problems of Language.* Peking: Foreign Language Press, 1976.

Steiner, George. *After Babel: Aspects of Language and Translation.* 3rd ed. OUP, 1998.

Subrhmanyam, Korada. *Theories of Language: Oriental and Occidental.* New Delhi: D.K.Printworld, 2008.

Tsetung, Mao. *Five Essays on Philosophy.* Peking: Foreign Languages Press, 1977.

Trask, R.L. *The Basics of Language.* Rpt. New Delhi: Foundation Books, 2003.

Krishnan Kutty

Wetherill, P.M. The *Literary Text: An Examination of Critical Methods.* Oxford: Basil Blackwell, 1974.

Williams, Raymond. *Marxism and Literature.* London: OUP, 1977.

.................*Key Words: A Vocabulary of Culture and Society.* Glasgow: Fontana, 1976.

Wimsatt, William K and Cleanth Brooks. *Literary Criticism: A Short History.* Calcutta: Oxford and IBH, 1967.

Zis, A. *Foundations of Marxist Aesthetics.* Moscow: Progress Publishers, 1977.

INDEX